EXTREME

NEW ENGLAND WEATHER

EXTREME

NEW ENGLAND WEATHER

BY JOSH JUDGE

Edited by Nikki Andrews
and Donna Judge

PUBLISHED BY SCIARTMEDIA
WWW.SCIARTMEDIA.COM

TABLE OF CONTENTS

PREFACE BY JOSH JUDGE

Although this book focuses on New England's extreme weather, it certainly isn't meant to imply that we constantly have "bad" conditions. Quite the contrary! As a lifelong New Englander, I think the area has some of the best weather in the world. Most of us choose to live in New England *because* of the four seasons that offer such a great variety.

It's never boring around here; we get to enjoy ever changing and constantly challenging forecasts. From beautiful blue skies, to pouring rains, picturesque snowstorms, and all that's in between, New England *can* (and usually *does*) provide almost every type of weather. You know the old saying, "if you don't like the weather in New England, wait a minute!"

This book sets out to examine the most extreme weather that visits our great region. After reading it, you'll have better insight into how these types of conditions manifest, how they affect us, and how you can be better prepared for them.

In addition, we'll take a look at some of the most infamous storms and weather events in our area's recent history. There have been so many thousands of extreme weather events, it isn't possible to recount them all, but hopefully we've covered some of the big ones you remember. I'm so proud to have assembled some of the best people in New England to help tell the stories of storms past, and I thank them for their time. I know you'll enjoy reading them.

The book has been written so you can read it in order, or seek out your favorite type of weather and read individual stand-alone chapters. After you're done, I hope it serves as a constant reference in times of stormy weather. A tropical storm is approaching? Just dig the book out and re-read the hurricane chapter. Scorching hot day? Check the all-time high temperatures for your state and see if you might break a record. Enjoy!

SPECIAL THANKS AND ACKNOWLEDGMENTS

First and foremost, I want to acknowledge my wife Donna, for suggesting the concept of including submissions from other New England meteorologists. That suggestion has made this book infinitely better.

Next, I am amazed by the fantastic contributions made by my colleagues all over the region. Thank you for your willingness to participate and for putting in some serious effort.

I'd also like to recognize: WMUR-TV, my employer, has also shown extreme support for my writing projects. Special thanks to Jeff Bartlett, Alisha McDevitt, and Maryann McDougall among others.

James Maynard, of SciArt Media who published this book, for his guidance and enthusiasm for the project.

The staff of the Mount Washington Observatory. They put a lot of work and effort into giving us a wonderful look into their daily lives.

Finally, all the great people who helped make this book so special with their photographs of weather events gone by. Special recognition to the the many state Departments of Emergency Management, as well as Glenn Martinsen for his help with these stunning images. It's really true, a picture is worth a thousand words... and with over 350 of them, this book is worth a LOT of words. Gathering so many pictures was quite a task, but dealing with some fantastic people along the way made it much more interesting.

Josh Judge

FOREWORD BY ELLIOT ABRAMS
Accuweather meteorologist and longtime New England radio forecaster

As the hurricane approached, the winds shifted. The boat was tossed against the rocks of a small island. Anthony Thatcher survived and climbed up the beach. Soon he saw his wife and rescued her, but where were their four children and other shipmates? They waited and peered into the darkness as massive waves bulldozed the beach. The wind screamed through the woods. But there were no more survivors. Today, Thatcher's Island appears as a speck on a map of the area around Cape Ann, MA. The island was named in memory of the tragic loss caused by the Great Colonial Hurricane of 1635.

They knew snow was coming, but it was dry during morning rush hour and the work and school day began. The snow arrived around midday and soon escalated into a whiteout. The first vehicles to get stuck blocked later traffic, and soon there was gridlock in the swirling blizzard. Harrowing rescues followed. By the time the blizzard of February 1978 was over, more than two feet had accumulated and the wind was forcing the snow into mammoth drifts.

The biggest snow storms of the winter of 2009-2010 missed New England, but buried Philadelphia under a seasonal record of more than 70 inches. But then came the early spring rains, and the teeming torrents made March go out like a swamp instead of a lamb. Unprecedented floods smashed through Rhode Island and parts of surrounding states.

After a cool summer in 2009, July of 2010 brought the furnace fires of grandiose grilling, the super searing, intensely igneous, fiercely firing and flaring, brazenly broiling pinnacle of perspiration: the summit of sweat and a surfeit of sultriness that is certainly sweltering. It is just that simple. It was almost as bad as the killer heat wave of July 1911.

As you start this fascinating book, there have been more storms and extreme weather changes. This is New England. Flanked by the Atlantic and the offshore Gulf Stream, the region rises from sea level to the majestic Green and White Mountains. It is within easy range of the bitter blusters from the remote frozen hinterlands of the Arctic, a land locked in snow and ice the year 'round, a land where the tender tundra is all too soon covered by the first snows of September, never to be seen again until the following June. Little wonder that New England is a crossroads in the vast highway of weather, and it has a penchant for extremes.

Here, in *Extreme New England Weather*, you'll meet a panel of 15 of New England's finest TV meteorologists as they convene with Josh Judge to tell their stories about a storm or extreme weather event they selected. This is the first compilation of its kind in New England, so breeze on in...

To my wife, Donna... Because she is my inspiration for all things...

Snow blowing after a big storm in Belfast, Maine. *Photo by Kevin Kratka*

CHAPTER 1: NOR'EASTERS, SNOWSTORMS AND BLIZZARDS

Some of the most memorable weather events in New England are the winter storms that bring amazing amounts of snow. You know-- the ones that take hours to shovel or snow-blow your driveway! They make getting from one place to another extremely difficult, or even impossible. The snow comes down fast and furious, and the wind blows it up against the windows, or snowdrifts pile up against the doors and walls of your house. These are the storms we remember the best through our life, and that's what we envision whenever somebody talks about a "snowstorm." How many memories do you have of staying in bed in anticipation, listening to the radio or watching TV to see if school was canceled? Some of these storms live up to the hype and some end up being a disappointment.

You've probably heard the terms "nor'easter" and "blizzard" thrown around hundreds of times, but what separates the two? Are they any different than a regular snowstorm? Is a blizzard worse than a nor'easter? Here's a look why different storms have specific names.

Nor'easters

Virtually everyone in New England has heard someone say, "Watch out, there's a nor'easter coming this week!" Just saying the name sends thousands of people to the grocery store to stock up on milk, bread, and other supplies. Does being a "nor'easter" mean the storm will be more fierce and destructive? Not necessarily, it simply describes the type of storm. Some are blockbusters and some move through with minimal impact, only turning stronger after they are far away from New England.

These storms sometimes cause confusion because of their name and the direction they travel from. Most often, they approach New England from the southwest or the south, causing people to wonder why we use the name "nor'easter" since they arrive from a different direction.

A nor'easter is named because of the direction the wind comes from as it passes by. It's just as simple as that. Oh, and nor'easters don't have to bring snow. They produce rain too. In fact, they often bring copious amounts of rain and wind in the spring or fall. In the winter, they usually include snow, as well as that nasty "rain/snow line."

Most large-scale organized storm systems have a wind circulation around them that moves in a counter-clockwise direction (in the northern hemisphere). A nor'easter also *usually* has a period of time where the wind is blowing FROM the northeast, because of that circulation around the storm center.

You be the Judge! ?

QUESTION: Dirty snow…

A) Causes traffic jams

B) Melts faster than clean snow

C) Tastes really bad

ANSWER: B (and probably C) – Dirty snow is darker, so it absorbs more of the sun's warmth, whereas clean snow reflects light.

Nor'easters can become exceptionally strong as they move over the Atlantic Ocean. This is usually caused as the cold air in a storm moves over the relatively warmer ocean waters, causing the two air masses to clash. Sometimes a seemingly weak storm to our south or west explodes into a powerful snow or rain storm as it passes us by several hours later. Often, these go on to become powerful ocean storms that have winds rivaling some tropical storms and hurricanes. When this happens, New England area meteorologists like to say the storm is "exploding," "bombing out," or that "bombogenesis" is occurring, because it *quickly explodes* into an amazingly strong storm.

Back in colonial days, satellite and radar equipment didn't exist, so people couldn't always tell which direction weather came from. When a rain or snowstorm moved in and the colonists noticed the wind blowing out of the northeast, they assumed that's where the storm was coming from. This is how the term "northeaster" is thought to have been born, often referred to by many New Englanders as a "nor'easter" (so that's what we'll call it in this book). Dropping the "th" in the word can be traced back hundreds of years to when people referred to points on a compass, using "nore" for north. It is thought (although there is some controversy about this) to have nothing to do with the New England regional dialect. If that were the case, we'd probably call it a "nah'eastah!" Actually, I think some people *do* call it that!

Blizzards

Not many people know the exact definition of a blizzard and just assume that it's a bad snowstorm. That is partly correct but there are some very specific things that must take place to earn this title. In short, the biggest variable is that your visibility is greatly reduced or completely gone. When the snow is coming down so hard that you can barely see in front of you, we say, "These are blizzard conditions." But are we right when we say that? Here are the official criteria that must be met:

- You must not be able to see beyond ¼ of a mile
- The wind must be sustained or frequently gusting to 35 mph or higher
- The above two conditions must happen for at least 3 hours

There are two ways blizzard conditions can develop. The first scenario is that it's snowing so heavily that you simply can't see through the falling snow very well and the wind is blowing above 35 mph. The second scenario is a bit more common in this part of the country. This is when a storm is pulling away and the wind picks up on the northwest side of the storm. Gusty winds from the northwest or west blow the snow up off the ground and into the air (sometimes called a "ground blizzard"). These conditions are usually accompanied by cold temperatures, meaning the snow is drier and lighter, and it is more easily picked up by the wind.

Attempting to drive through blizzard conditions can be dangerous, and even life-threatening. Traveling through a "whiteout," or blowing and drifting snow, means you can't see anything ahead of you, including other cars or turns in the road.

Blizzards also usually mean very cold temperatures, made even worse by the "wind chill factor," which is how cold the air feels to exposed skin. People stuck in blizzard conditions can face frostbite and even hypothermia.

During a blizzard, visibility is lowered significantly, making travel very dangerous. Staying under this speed limit shouldn't be a problem!

When you think about the second type of conditions above, you realize that it's possible for a blizzard to even occur when it is NOT snowing and the skies are clear! The only requirement is that the wind is blowing the snow around and you can't see above a quarter mile for at least 3 hours.

Snowstorms

A snowstorm is simply a generic term for any weather system that drops a moderate to sizeable amount of snow. Technically, a nor'easter can also be snowstorm, and even a blizzard – as long as it's the kind of blizzard where it is actually snowing. For more information on winter weather awareness and interesting facts, go online to: *www.nws.noaa.gov/om/winter/index.shtml*

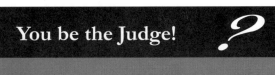

You be the Judge!

QUESTION: On a sunny day with snow all around you, it is possible to...

A) See better than normal

B) Get a sunburn

C) Melt it all with a magnifying glass

ANSWER: B - When snow is all around on a sunny day, the white snow can reflect the sunlight and cause a sunburn.

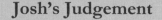

Josh's Judgement

So you see, it's actually possible to have a snowstorm, blizzard, and nor'easter all the same time!

Snow Squalls

You can almost think of snow squalls as "mini blizzards." They often satisfy most of the requirements except they don't last long enough to qualify. They are intense areas of snow that move in quickly, changing things from quiet to heavy snowfall in minutes. Snow squalls can drop several inches of snow in short bursts, often coming down at a rate of 2 to 5 inches per hour! This can be very dangerous for drivers as these conditions spawn quickly and can reduce or eliminate visibility. Winds usually pick up suddenly in conjunction with the snow, creating whiteout conditions. Many multi-car accidents occur as a squall moves in on unsuspecting motorists.

Here in New England, squalls most often form along a strong cold front that's moving through. The intense change in temperature and wind direction causes incredible instability in much the same way a thunderstorm forms along a front in warmer weather.

Snow squalls can spoil a weather forecaster's day when they move through and drop much more snow than expected. Sometimes people wake up to three to five freshly fallen inches of snow when they were expecting little or none. They are also very "scattered" and "hit and miss" in nature (just like thunderstorms), meaning that they can blitz one town and miss the next.

Record Snow Storms for Select New England Cities		
Source: National Weather Service		
Burlington, VT	33.1"	Jan 2-3, 2010
Worcester, MA	33.0"	March 31 - April 1, 1997
Providence, RI	28.6"	Feb 6-7, 1978
Boston, MA	27.5"	Feb 18-19, 2003
Concord, NH	27.5"	March 11-13, 1888
Portland, ME	27.1"	Jan 17-18, 1979
Hartford, CT	21.9"	Feb 12, 2006

After a 1960 snow storm in Boston, it was easier to travel down Beacon Hill on skis!

Photo by Nick DeWolf

The snow comes down fast and furious in downtown Boston in 1958.

Photo by Nick DeWolf

There's a lot of snow to shovel on Boston's Commonwealth Avenue.

Courtesy the Northeast River Forecast Center

Clearing the roads after a big snowfall in Savoy, Massachusetts.

Photo: MassDOT

Snow is usually welcome for the first month or two... and then some people start getting a bit sick of it. Here's a way to make it more tolerable.

SNOWIEST AND LEAST SNOWY WINTERS ON RECORD				
Source: National Weather Service				
	MOST		LEAST	
Burlington, VT	145.4"	1970-71	31.3"	1912-13
Worcester, MA	132.9"	1995-96	21.2"	1954-55
Concord, NH	122.0"	1873-74	27.0"	1979-80
Hartford, CT	115.2"	1995-96	14.7"	1936-37
Boston, MA	107.6"	1995-96	8.2"	1936-37
Portland, ME	107.6"	1970-71	9.5"	1936-37
Providence, RI	106.1"	1995-96	8.9"	1997-98

Types of snow

Why does some snow feel "heavy and wet" and some feel "light and fluffy?" Many people have asked that question as they struggled to shovel their driveway clear of a wet and pasty snow that seemed like concrete. On the other hand, kids complain when a fluffy and dry snow doesn't allow them to make a good snowman or snowball to throw at their unsuspecting friends.

The reason all comes down to *temperature.* When the temperature of the air is *colder*, the snow is light, dry, and fluffy. Generally for lighter snow, temperatures need to be in the teens and 20s (Fahrenheit) during the snowfall.

Higher temperatures when it's snowing, usually in the 30s, mean a snowfall that is heavier, stickier, and wetter.

Why?

Because of a simple meteorological rule: cold air can't hold as much water as warmer air. If temperatures are colder, snow (produced up in the clouds) doesn't have as much water to work with, so much more *air* goes into the snowflakes. On the other hand, when the temperatures are

If you love snow, you probably love to go outside and measure it! Make sure you do it in an area that is out in the open, away from buildings, and take several measurements in different locations to confirm your findings.

higher, there's a lot of moisture in the clouds. In this case, the snow becomes heavier because there's a lot more water (and less air) in each and every flake.

A heavy, wet snow covers Quincy Market in Boston.

Photo by AntyDiluvian

APPROXIMATE MELT WATER EQUIVALENT

How much snow does one inch of water make? It depends on the temperature!

28° to 34° makes about 10" of snow

20° to 27° makes about 15" of snow

15° to 19° makes about 20" of snow

10° to 14° makes about 30" of snow

zero° to 9° makes about 40" of snow

-20° to -1° makes about 50" of snow

-40° to -21° makes about 100" of snow

Precipitation types

Often when a winter weather system moves through our region, some areas receive the infamous "wintry mix," while others get just snow or rain. Why the difference? There are various reasons depending on each storm, but they usually involve one of these explanations.

- A warm front arrives from our south, bringing warmer air and a shift in wind direction, often from the south or southwest, which changes the snow over to rain or ice.

- When winds blow onto land from the relatively warmer ocean water, this sets up a smaller warm front called a *coastal front*. Even in the middle of winter, our Atlantic Ocean temperatures are usually above 32° Fahrenheit, so when the wind comes from over the ocean it is usually warmer. When these warmer winds come ashore, they can change snow over to rain. This is why coastal areas so often receive rain or lower snow amounts than areas farther inland. As this milder air moves inland, it gradually cools down. This is where the rain/snow line sets up. How far inland this happens is determined by the temperature of the Atlantic, how strong the wind is, or the track the storm takes.

Notable Snowstorms & Stories

The Blizzard of 1888, March 11 – At the time it was referred to as "The White Hurricane." It is one of the biggest snow storms in recorded history. The winter appeared to be over and people were beginning to think spring. Crocuses were already popping up, farmers had begun to prepare their fields, and temperatures had turned quite mild. A light rain broke out that day, not alarming anyone until it began to change to snow, and then a blinding snow! It was a three-day event that blanketed New England (and the entire northeast) with some locations measuring 40 to 50 inches of snow and up to 30-foot drifts! Winds blasted at 80 mph while temperatures fell well below zero. Over 400 people died and countless others were injured from frostbite, exhaustion from the cleanup, and the hardships of so much snow. Life came to a standstill and supplies ran low, as most food and coal was brought in by trains, which couldn't run through the snow. Telegraph lines were downed, rendering communication with other areas impossible. The storm also had a major effect on much of New York and New Jersey. New York City received around 22 inches which halted virtually everything. One positive outcome in the Boston area was that the storm convinced officials of the need for underground utilities and services, and led to the construction of the nation's first subway system.

Approximate snow totals from the blizzard of 1888.

Mountains of snow in New Britain, Connecticut.

Taking a break from shoveling out from the blizzard of 1888 in Keene, NH. Snow banks were much higher than the people shoveling!

Courtesy Keene NH Library

Bridgeport, Ct: Looking up State Street after the big blizzard. The piles make it hard to see very far.

Courtesy Bridgeport Public Library

Keene, NH: Looks like trouble! Not quite enough room in this snow path for people (and animals) going different directions.

Taking a quick break from the shoveling in Keene, because when 40 to 50 inches of snow falls, you'll be shoveling for a while.

Trains were the main way that supplies were delivered at the time. This locomotive crashed in the amazingly high snow after the blizzard.

Photo courtesy NOAA Photo Library

Valentine's Day - Feb 14, 1940 - Tallies were over a foot of a pasty wet snow that took extra strength to lift with a shovel. The storm was especially notable because of the effect it had on the transportation system, particularly in Boston. Highways were jam packed and bus and train stations were closed. According to the Boston Globe, over 10,000 people were forced to spend the night at Boston's North Station. Several babies were born while in transit, unable to reach the hospital.

Cleaning up from the 1940 storm in Boston. A Valentine's Day gift to remember!

The Mohawk Trail (Route 2) between Greenfield and North Adams, MA after the big snowfall from the Valentine's Day Blizzard of 1940.

Photo by Marion Post Wolcott

Feb-Mar 1947 – A busy two-month stretch of winter storms, one of which produced 16 straight days of snow! Parts of central Massachusetts racked up four-foot totals.

After sixteen straight days of snow, a lot of it can pile up, like it did in western Massachusetts in 1947.

March 1956 Etrusco Storm – After a fairly quiet winter for snowfall, a change of events was in the cards for New England. No less than three nor'easters within a 10-day stretch dumped heavy amounts of snow in our backyards. The second storm, on March 16th and 17th, is famous in the town of Scituate, MA because the Italian freighter *Etrusco* was grounded by rough seas March 16 on Cedar Point. The 7,000-ton, 444-foot-long cargo ship was headed to Boston to pick up a load of grain that it was to deliver to Romania.

A painting of the freighter, Etrusco, which grounded at Cedar Point in Scituate, Ma. This was painted from a photo that was taken of Alden and Richard Finnie sitting on the rocks and looking at the ship as it sat helplessly.

Photo courtesy Heath Finnie, painted by Olga Finnie

Featured Contributor

Heavy snow fell at Boston's Logan airport, making piles of work for cleaning crews.

Photo copyright Bob Copeland 1956-2010

Memories of the 1956 *Etrusco* Snowstorm

Meteorologist Bob Copeland, formerly WCVB-TV, Boston

The winter of 1955-56 had been very frustrating from a snow-lover's point of view, with essentially no storms worth talking about. But March 1956, at the tail end of winter, was to be different, with three major snowstorms hitting the Boston area before the month was finished.

I was a first-year graduate student at MIT at the time, and in the weather lab we were following this perfect coastal storm scenario on Friday, March 16. A strong arctic high was centered just north of New England, the primary low in the Ohio Valley was weakening as upper level energy shifted to a

warm front along the North Carolina coast and the results were amazing. By 1:30AM on Saturday, March 17th the "secondary" low center was already 50 miles east of Nantucket and racing away, but it had deepened 46 millibars (very strong) in 24 hours - qualifying as "bombogenesis" according to my MIT thesis advisor, the late Prof. Fred Sanders, who loved these events just as much as I did.

My recollection is that we received at least 18" of snow around Cambridge but the wind blew with gusts over 60 mph during the storm so the snow was badly drifted. The gale also drove the freighter *Etrusco* onto the rocky shoreline at Scituate, and the storm became known for a time as the "*Etrusco* Storm." I heard reports of massive snowdrifts at Logan Airport and I convinced my MIT friend and renowned cloud physicist, the late Dr. Reginald Newell, to accompany me to the airport to check it out. We made our way to Logan via the MTA and what we found when we got to the old International Terminal was astounding. Although Boston's official observation for the storm was less than a foot of snow, my pictures suggest that the wind must have blown much of the precipitation past the gauges and deposited it all near the terminal, where drifts of 8 to 12 *feet* were common. In one of the images, you can see where the plows had to stop. The runways and the ramps had been cleared, but the enormous job of removing tons of snow near the gates was left to humans with shovels. One final meteorological note - with gales off the ocean, temperatures at Logan were very close to 32° F during much of the storm, meaning that the snow was very wet. But the combination of wet snow and 60 mph winds sculpted these huge meringue-like snowdrifts the likes of which I have not seen before or since!

(See pictures)

Amazingly tall and interestingly shaped snow drifts abound around Logan Airport in the 1956 Etrusco storm.

Photos copyright Bob Copeland 1956-2010.

February 1969, aka "The Hundred-Hour Snowstorm" – There were two major storms in February. One of them brought a record 101 straight hours of snowfall and dropped 26.3" in Boston (a record high snowfall at the time, but now the 3rd ranked measurement). Snow began early on the 24th and didn't stop until midday on the 28th, leaving snow drifts higher than 10 feet tall on many major highways.   Particularly hard hit was Boston's north shore, as well as northern New Hampshire and Maine, all of these areas seeing between three and five feet accumulation. Some of New Hampshire's White Mountains received anywhere from 70" to Mount Washington's amazing 98-inch snowfall.

These two photos from Quincy, Mass show how much snow was on the ground in February, 1969 once it finally stopped falling!

Photos provided by Jeff and Jan Towne.

ABOVE: Standing next to all that snow in Quincy, Massachusetts after the "Hundred-Hour Snowstorm."

RIGHT: And of course kids with shovels are valuable helpers.

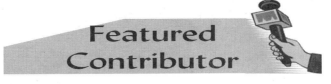

Featured Contributor

Starting my career off with a bang!

Meteorologist Bruce Schwoegler, former WBZ-TV, Boston

New England's heralded "wait a minute" weather was no surprise to me, a rookie broadcast meteorologist embarking on what came to be a three and a half decade TV romp through the vagaries of atmospheric aerobatics so commonplace in the region. Heading a team of analysts and forecasters for the North Pacific and Arctic from Fleet Weather Central based at Naval Air Station Kodiak, Alaska, I had already honed my post-university forecasting skills. A subsequent post at Fleet Weather Facility in Jacksonville, Florida, added tropical experience related to surface and aircraft operations in the Atlantic and Caribbean. Both proved to be of value in forecasting the 1969 snow event, 6,000 "wait a minutes," for an audience that dwarfed today's standards.

Like folks in endless supermarket lines before a storm, everyone eagerly awaited check out of the 1969 snows and winds. Some forecasts indicated an end in two days. Persistence proved them wrong. So did expertise in evaluating surface and upper air weather data. Such notions are born from experience and knowledge imparted by previous storms. These "seat of the pants" inclinations remain important factors in forecasting skill despite advanced modeling and the more recent additions of slick computer graphic futures. I was fortunate in that my meteorology career invoked both the old and the new since it commenced during the

infancy of mathematical models, sophisticated radar and high resolution satellite data. My colleague and morning TV meteorologist, Don Kent, added localized nuggets to my repertoire.

Freshly fallen snow in Gray, Maine.

Photo by Dan Burgess

Together, we disseminated weather forecasts that utilized relatively sparse but important data that enabled us to state that the four-day storm would continue. Factors like the persistence and positioning of a Canadian high pressure area relative to a developing low pressure system just to our south entered the mix. An extensive "fetch," a term denoting moist surface airflow from south of Newfoundland back toward New England, did too. Its upslope journey onto New England's landscape fed outrageous snowfalls. Until changes became evident, my evening weathercasts were simply, "The snow and wind will continue." They did - in record proportions. I had arrived only months earlier, in the fall of 1968, and it was my Boston and broadcasting baptism under fire, a legacy that would continue through the Blizzard of 1978 and many storms beyond.

"The Blizzard of '78", Feb. 6 & 7th – It's the "big one" that people still talk about to this day. Infamous for combining heavy snowfall, blinding blizzard conditions, and coastal flooding, it lasted nearly 36 hours and paralyzed the entire region for a week! Snowfall amounts were amazing, with drifts up to 27 feet high in Rhode Island. Check out some of these tallies:

Rockport, MA: 32.5"

Woonsocket, RI: 28"

Providence, RI: 28.6"

Boston, MA: 27.1" (2nd all-time highest snowfall)

Worcester, MA: 20.2"

Hartford, CT: 16.9"

Nearly 5,500 cars in New England were stranded and abandoned on major highways for days, the National Guard was mobilized, and houses were destroyed by battering waves and flooding. Winds were up to hurricane strength, gusting at 79 mph in Boston and 93 mph at Chatham on Cape Cod. Ninety-nine people were killed, seventy-three of them in Massachusetts and twenty-six in Rhode Island.

Believe it or not, this storm was not a surprise! It was forecast quite well, with a *winter storm watch* posted thirty hours before and a *heavy snow warning* not long after that. The problem, according the National Weather Service, was that people were skeptical because there had been a series of somewhat inaccurate forecasts leading up to the blizzard.

Digging the cars out on Route 128. Thousands of cars were stranded for days.

Photo copyright Bob Copeland 1978-2010. Used with permission.

The Blizzard of '78 left over two feet in Boston. Here are some amazing shots from the Back Bay area just after the snow stopped falling.

Photos by Eric Pence

Quincy, MA – After the blizzard, snow banks were so high that you really had to search for the people (look closely).

Photo courtesy Jackie Fritsche

Revere, MA – Once the snow and wind stopped, people emerged to see the new winter wonderland.

Photo by John J. O'Brien

Storm surge from the blizzard pounds coastal homes in Scituate, Mass.

Photo from the NOAA Photo Library

Blizzard of '78 - Coastal damage in Massachusetts

Waterfront buildings covered with sand and debris in Rockport.

In Nahant, so much sand was washed onto the road that snowplows were brought in to get rid of it.

The Rockport shoreline in ruins.

A north shore house that was destroyed by the storm surge.

Photos by Joe Pelczarski, courtesy of the Massachusetts Office of Coastal Zone Management, www.mass.gov/czm/blizzard78.htm

The Blizzard of '78

Meteorologist Harvey Leonard – WCVB-TV, Boston

27.1" of snow in Boston. 28.6" of snow in Providence. Hurricane force wind gusts producing drifts over 15 feet high in Massachusetts! 3500 vehicles stuck along Route 128 alone. Fourteen of the many people trapped in those vehicles died, presumably from carbon monoxide poisoning when they left their motors running to try to stay warm while snow piled up above the level of their exhaust systems. A total of 99 deaths were attributed to the storm in Massachusetts & Rhode Island. There were massive power outages and record high tides, with huge waves on top that crumbled sea walls and devastated coastal communities, leaving many homeless. The National Guard was called in to rescue folks and to help with the massive job of snow removal. Southern New England was shut down for a full week!

It was The Blizzard of '78, and it became the winter storm by which all others are measured. Anyone old enough to remember it will never forget it. Those too young to remember, or who weren't born yet, have listened to amazing accounts of the storm from their parents and/or grandparents. Each person who was around has his or her own compelling story to tell, and that includes meteorologists who were working the storm.

It was my first winter forecasting on Boston television, after having spent three years on Providence television. The winter of 1977-1978 had already been a very eventful and active one. On Friday, January 20, 1978, just a few weeks before The Blizzard of '78, a powerful winter nor'easter struck, producing 21" of snow in just 12 hours in Boston, with wind gusts over 50 mph. Surely, I thought, that would be the most powerful storm of the winter. But, I was proven wrong just two and a half weeks later.

The Blizzard of '78 began early on Monday, February 6th and the snow did not stop falling until Tuesday night, the 7th. But for me it really began days earlier.

I was the weekend and weekday noon meteorologist at Channel 7 in Boston at the time, but our chief meteorologist, Dr. Fred Ward was away the Thursday and Friday before the storm, so I was filling in. It was on that Thursday, February 2nd, that I began to suspect that the forces of nature might be aligning to produce something very major several days down the road.

A large and bitter cold high pressure area was centered just north of Minnesota, bringing frigid temperatures to the northern states, including New England. Meanwhile, some of our computer models were indicating that a strong disturbance at high levels of the atmosphere would drop down out of Alberta Province in Canada (we call these disturbances Alberta Clippers), and move through the lower Great Lakes over the weekend, and then reach the East Coast on Monday. These storms normally carry only limited moisture--until they reach the East Coast, where they can then tap into the vast moisture source we know as the Atlantic Ocean.

Now, it's important to note that in the 1970s weather computer models were not nearly as sophisticated or as accurate as they are today. As a forecaster, one would really have to make use of his or her education and experience to make great leaps of faith from what the computer models were indicating to what actually might happen. I began to realize that this might be just such a case.

Ever since I was a little boy, I was fascinated by weather, especially storms, and most especially winter storms. I was so into winter storms, that through the years, I was building a mental encyclopedia of all winter storms. So, even back in 1978, I considered winter storms to be my area of greatest interest and ability.

Even though computer models were only hinting at a significant storm, I had seen enough to feel fairly confident that we would be in for a biggie.

First, bitter cold air was already established. Second, the ocean water temperature was cold (35-36 degrees). This is important, because many of these types of storms can result in a change to rain, especially along the coast as ocean winds increase, if ocean water temperatures are higher. Third, based on my experience with computer models at the time, I knew they underestimated the strength of these storms when they reach the East Coast. And, fourth, we were in a very active winter pattern which favored many East Coast storms. I knew then, as I know now, that when we are in such a pattern, we usually have multiple major nor'easters in a winter season. Conversely, when we are not in such a pattern, we can sometimes go the entire winter season without ever getting a major snowstorm.

So, with all of this in mind, I went on the air Thursday night, February 2nd , four days before the storm, and said that the potential was there for a major snowstorm early the following week. I also remember saying, "But one doesn't want to go too far out on a limb, or one may fall off." In those days, forecasting a potential major snowstorm four days before was virtually unheard of.

On Friday night, February 3rd, my confidence grew stronger on the air, and by Saturday night, February 4th, I was about as convinced as a forecaster could be, considering it was still 36 hours before the expected start of the storm.

I remember all of this as if it was yesterday. I was so worked up that I could hardly sleep from Thursday night on, meaning that by the time the storm actually began on Monday the 6th, I was already exhausted!

But, as confident as I was on the air in the days before the storm, as soon as I left the station and began to think, I would get really nervous. What if something goes wrong? After all, this is weather, and even today, there are still occasional surprises that cause forecasts to go awry. In those days, that would happen considerably more often. After making such a strong call on the storm on Saturday night, February 4th, I worried that if anything did go wrong, I would probably be run out of town. After all, it was just my first winter forecasting on Boston television. My wife can tell you that I wasn't easy to live before that storm hit. I was so obsessed with the potential storm that I could not concentrate on anything else!

I was off the day before the storm hit (Sunday February 5th). My wife (six months pregnant at the time) and I went out with some friends that day. But I was really somewhere else, in my own world, imagining the impact this storm was going to have, while still fearing something might go wrong.

I was scheduled to work the next day (Monday, February 6th) both in the morning and at noon. But I couldn't wait that long to get to work. I kissed my wife good-bye at 11:30 PM Sunday night and headed into the station. Little did I know at the time that it would be a full week before I would see her again. I just had to be where the action was, and most importantly, where all the weather information would be. (Remember this was before the days of the internet, so I couldn't study the weather situation unless I was actually in the workplace.)

I tried to sleep on a couch at the station for a few hours, but my mind would not settle down enough to allow that, so I just watched the limbs on the trees sway to and fro as the northeasterly winds gradually increased. Then I went into the weather center to start checking the latest data. All looked good, as snow was stretching from Washington to Bridgeport, Connecticut. The temperature was 25° in Boston, which was fine, but then in just one hour the temperature jumped to 30° as the wind became more easterly and increased further. Oh

no! Did this mean that Boston would wind up with rain and I would look like the biggest fool in the world? Would my career be over at the young age of twenty-nine? Fortunately, it did not. The ocean was cold enough to keep it all snow (except on Cape Cod, which did experience a change to rain). It did mean that coastal areas would have a wetter snow, while inland areas would have a dry powdery snow, what we would call a powder blizzard.

Cars covered in snow in downtown Boston after The Blizzard of '78.

Photo courtesy Eric Pence

Some ocean-effect snow flurries began in Boston around 10 AM and by noontime a steady light snow was falling. But at 5 PM there was still just a light snow falling, and Boston only had less than 1" of accumulation, while Providence already had over 6". Did this mean that at the last minute the storm was moving out to sea a bit too far south to nail Boston? These are the fears a forecaster has when his forecast, and in this case, his reputation, as well as his career, are on the line. Well, just as my anxiety reached a peak, the snow began to rapidly increase in intensity in Boston, and The Blizzard of '78 was really underway.

Harvey Leonard (shown here broadcasting The Blizzard of '78) is currently Chief Meteorologist at WCVB-TV in Boston, MA, and has been privileged to have a 36-year career as a television meteorologist in New England, including the last 33 years in Boston.

SURVIVING EXTREME WEATHER

Didn't Desire to Doze Near Death!

by Rella Bartlett

I was nineteen years old and working at AT&T in North Andover, Mass. We were let out early due to the storm. I had a friend who asked me for a ride home. It took us two and half hours to get to Haverhill, normally a 15-minute drive. Did I mention she lived in a funeral home? When we got to her house she asked me up, and said I could not drive to Plaistow, NH. I went upstairs, naive as I was; her dad told me I could stay in the guest room. All of a sudden I heard this ungodly noise. I didn't want to look like a fool so I politely asked, "What was that?" Her dad said that there was a body he had just brought in! I got on the phone, called my dad and said, "You have to come get me NOW." I waited out in my car two more hours for him to get there, and then it took another three hours to get from Haverhill to Plaistow! I had no car for three weeks, but it was worth the aggravation.

October 31, 1991 Halloween Nor'easter - AKA "The No-Name Storm" or "The Perfect Storm," and it's the one that inspired a book of that name by Sebastian Junger, and later a movie. The title was coined by the National Weather Service while Junger interviewed them, in which they told him that in order to spawn a storm of this magnitude, conditions had to be "perfect." These "perfect" ingredients were: a cold front coming from the west and the remnants of former Hurricane Grace. The two combined to make a hybrid storm referred to as "extra-tropical," which came very close to New England (just off Cape Cod). As the storm pulled away over the Atlantic, it actually became a new hurricane, with winds of 75 mph and it later went on to make landfall over coastal Canada. For whatever the reason, this hurricane was never named, thus the "No-Name Storm" nickname. The Halloween Nor'easter is blamed for 12 deaths, and millions of dollars in damage.

The raging ocean waves from "The Perfect Storm," pounding the rocks in Rockland, Mass.

Photo by John Gerraughty

The No-Name Storm
Meteorologist Dick Albert, longtime personality WCVB-TV, Boston

I live for storms. I've always been excited when nature acted up. The perfect example was the so called "No-Name Storm" on Halloween, October 31st, 1991. The "Perfect Storm" was so perfect because all the atmospheric ingredients came together to create such a giant storm.

I remember closely watching the computer models, the satellite pictures and all the incoming data. I remember thinking, "I've never seen anything like this before." This monster was forming near Nova Scotia and moving westward, (a highly unusual direction) towards New England.

Massive waves would be generated. A Canadian buoy reported a wave height of 100 feet! Could this be true? I thought about the hurricane gusts, the pounding of the waves, the coastal damage and the beach erosion from Cape Cod to Cape Ann to Camden, Maine.

We asked Channel 5 viewers to send in their videos of the storm. I couldn't believe the size of the waves smashing the shoreline in Scituate and Revere, and the house falling into the ocean in Chatham. Another viewer sent in a home movie of waves, at least 30 feet high, rolling into Perkins Cove in Ogunquit, Maine. Having spent many summers in Ogunquit, I knew this was a rare event indeed.

I have always believed that the "No-Name Storm" should have been named Hurricane Henri. It totally fit the description of a true hurricane. This "Perfect Storm" should have been put into the record books along with the other famous New England hurricanes: the '38 Hurricane, Carol, Edna and Bob.

March 12-14, 1993, AKA the "Super storm" and "The storm of the century" – It was a major snowstorm that left tall snow banks all the way up the East Coast. At the time it was called the "Blizzard of the Century," because of its amazingly large reach. For the first time ever, every airport on the East Coast was closed down at one time or another. Much of New England was covered in one to two feet of snow, with northern New Hampshire measuring the most, including Lincoln, NH's 35 inches, the highest in the region. Wind blew the snow into even higher drifts, up to 10 feet. Boston's wind gusted to 81 mph and atop Mount Washington winds were clocked at 144 mph.

A satellite view of the 1993 "Storm of the Century." Notice how large it was, reaching from south to north.

April Fools' Day Storm 1997: It was no prank, this storm meant business! Despite the fact that the previous day had been in the 50s and lower 60s (quite warm for late March), things turned on a dime. It began on March 31st and ended on April 1st. Boston piled up 25.4" of snowfall and although this is not a record total, it was the highest snowfall Boston has ever received in a 24-hour period. Worcester, MA stacked up 33", which still stands as their highest storm total ever. There was up to three feet in other parts of New England as well.

Featured Contributor

The April Fool's Day Snow Storm
Meteorologist David Brown, WCVB-TV, Boston

The winter of 1996-1997 was shaping up to be a cake walk. The end of March was just around the corner and Boston had only picked up 25 inches of snow. Quite a difference from the previous winter of 1995-1996, which was my first as a meteorologist at WCVB in Boston, and it was record setter. 107.6 inches of snow fell that season, starting early in December and falling often afterwards as well. That was my introduction to forecasting, to living, and to getting to work by 3:30 in the morning.

I was the morning meteorologist at CVB and no matter what, had to get to work by 3:30 am. If there was an impending blizzard I could sleep at a nearby hotel. No worries.

This brings me to Friday, March 28th. I was working for chief Meteorologist Dick Albert. On that day the GFS (Global Forecast System) Long Range Computer model had a strong storm forecast to develop and hit Southern New England on Tuesday April 1. I remember putting together my five-day forecast. I hinted at a blizzard on Day 4 of the 5-day, but chuckled and said, "Wouldn't that be a funny April Fools' Day joke?" An actual blizzard on that day in a season that wasn't snowy at all.

April Fools! The day before, Carlisle, MA reached 60 degrees and the next day it looked like this!

Photo courtesy Lin Xu

On Sunday March 30th, Easter Sunday, the weather could not have been more lovely. There was abundant sunshine, a high temperature of 63 degrees, and my neighbors had started their spring clean up of in their flower beds. I yelled across the yard to Debbie. "You may want to wait on that. In fact if I were you I'd gas up your snowblower." The forecast was calling for a snowstorm on the 1st, but people weren't listening. Debbie shrugged her shoulders and said her husband was in charge of shoveling.

On Monday, the final day of March, the month was just about to go out as a lion. A cold front passed, our temperature dropped into the 40s and the southern branch of the jet stream was helping a low pressure system develop to our south.

Winter Storm Warnings were posted. By the noon show on WCVB I was the lead. I popped up at the beginning of the news saying that Boston could see up to two feet of snow. Don't you love some of those qualifying words: "could" and "up to?" While I was looking down the barrel of a major snowstorm, I was also thinking of the climate of the season. Boston had never seen a snowstorm like this. Was I ready to pull the trigger and forecast a blizzard of record proportions? I felt confident and comfortable saying two feet of snow could fall. In fact later that afternoon, on our five o'clock forecast, chief meteorologist Dick Albert was forecasting the same.

During the day the storm started to intensify off the coast of Maryland and with cold air coming down from the north what started off as rain began to mix with wet snow. By noon it was all snow.

Just before I left for the afternoon my boss, our news director, asked if I wanted to sleep in the hotel. "No," I said. "I had no problem getting in last winter, I won't have a problem getting in tomorrow morning. I'll leave early, but I'll make it." That was the wrong decision. Who could have guessed that just 12 hours from then I would embark on a journey that would require me to abandon my car, hitch a ride with a snowplow operator, and drive to work in the jeep of a Boston Police officer.

By 7 that night I was in bed. My alarm was set for 1 AM. At 11 PM I heard the sound that every winter-loving meteorologist yearns to hear in a snow storm: thunder! I woke up, looked out the window and saw the snow coming down fast and furious. Even in the darkness of near midnight I could tell the snow was pasted and painted over every surface. I would learn later that from 7 PM to 11 PM the snow fell at a rate of at least an inch per hour. During the peak of the storm from 11 PM until 3 AM, snow fell at an almost unheard of rate of three inches per hour, some of the heaviest Boston had ever seen.

I looked out the window, yawned deeply, and muttered to myself that I probably should get to work. I turned on the news and as I thought, a major blizzard was underway, heavy wet snow was falling. I must say it is one thing to understand this from a meteorological and atmospheric perspective, but I was just about to experience firsthand the effect of the major blizzard.

I was out the door, all showered, and ready to go by 11:50. I would have several hours to get to work and get on the air. Little did I know that I would need every minute of travel time and only get to work with 9 minutes to spare.

I went to get in my car and back up, but only got four to five feet. I tried to shovel my car out of the driveway, but the thick cement-like snow was not budging. Looking down my street and noticing the downed power line and live wires, I knew that even if I was to get out of the driveway I would never make it down the road.

My street emptied out to the major roadway, one which been plowed, but was accumulating snow quickly. I grabbed my briefcase and sport coat and waded through the waist-deep snow to the parkway to find an idling snowplow.

"Hey there, aren't you the weather guy?" bellowed the operator. "Yeah, I need to get to work. Can you drive me?" "Sorry pal," said the operator, "I can't leave city streets. Not allowed to cross over to Needham. I can take you to the police station, perhaps they can give you a ride."

It seemed like good idea; at least I'd be heading in the right direction. I only needed to travel 5.7 miles from my house to work.

I arrived at the police station and endured the laughs that the weather guy was stranded, but felt reassured that one of Boston's Finest would be escorting me to work. The time now was 1:45 AM. I had 3 hours and 15 minutes to get to work and on the air.

Officer Roberts and I climbed into his 4-wheel drive Jeep and started driving down the parkway to Route 128. At the first stop light a huge 40-foot spruce was downed by the weight of the snow. We slowly, deliberately, and methodically moved through the sludge of snow, traveling between 8 and 15 miles per hour. I knew I wouldn't have much time to spare but that I would arrive at the studio. This thought changed once I hit 128. Although it was already 4 AM and I only had one mile to go, traffic was stuck. It was the proverbial parking lot. The snow was still falling, cars were not moving, and I was on the phone with the producer of the morning show.

"Jen, I'm only a mile away, but traffic is not moving." With that said, cars started slowly moving. Time was ticking. For the first time in four hours I could breathe! I saw exit 19 approach, the turn-off for Channel 5.

The time was 4:51 AM, 9 minutes until air time. It had already been a marathon to get to the station. I got set for 7 hours of continuous coverage of one of the worst blizzards to ever affect New England.

During the morning coverage we learned that the snow came down too fast for road crews to keep up; many roads remained impassable for days. Boston's transit system was hit hard. The "T" could not run above ground, buses also stayed off the streets. Air travel was also grounded for days because of the storm. The heavy and wet snow caused tree limbs and even whole trees to fall, downing many power lines in the process. Electricity was knocked out for nearly 700,000 people.

Officially Boston picked up 25.4 inches of snow over two days. This was the 3rd biggest snowstorm for the city, the heaviest late season snowstorm and a record for 24-hour snowfall, and it officially wasn't even a winter storm. Towns outside of Boston picked up more. On April 3rd, temperatures reached the 50s and we had 70s within a week. While the snow melted, the memories last for the April Fools' Storm, so much that thirteen years later, for this meteorologist, it seems like yesterday.

The March Blizzard that Missed Its Mark

Chief Meteorologist Tom Messner, WPTZ, Burlington, Vt

The storm that formed in the Western Gulf of Mexico on Saturday, March 3, 2001 had all the right ingredients to be a big one for East Coast metropolitan areas. Excited meteorologists went on television in New York and Philadelphia, warning viewers that the snow would be measured in feet – not inches – when the storm hit.

And by all rights, they should have been shoveling, come Monday. Except that storms don't always perform the way the computer models say they will, and this one proved to be the undoing of many a forecaster.

What happened? When the storm first formed, it looked like a whopper. Then came the second low pressure system along the Mid-Atlantic Coast, creating the perfect ingredients for a classic nor'easter. A high pressure system over Northern New England should have ensured that the storm hovered over New York and Philadelphia for a good long time, dumping snow as predicted.

But ultimately, when that nor'easter formed, it developed farther north than the computer models had suggested, and the predictions of "historic snowfall" for New York and Philadelphia fell way short. The snow that did fall was measured in inches, rather than feet. New York City's famed Central Park ended up with a measly three and a half inches of slushy snow, most of which melted shortly after it fell. And the meteorologists who had predicted the monster snowfall? They were getting the cold shoulder.

In fact, NBC's *Today Show* went so far as to launch a tongue-in-cheek investigation. Just where did Al Roker's two feet of snow end up falling? They found the answer to their question right here in the Champlain Valley, which got the brunt of the storm that swung north of the city. Burlington, VT saw twenty-three inches of snow, while Lake Placid, NY was buried under thirty-five inches, and Jay Peak, VT received a full three feet during the Monday-Tuesday storm.

Two days later, while we were still digging out, the *Today Show* set up a live shot with us just outside the WPTZ-TV studios. They wanted to see snow. We knew how to deliver. I greeted Katie Couric and Matt Lauer live on national television, waving with my shovel from the top of a parking lot snow bank that was nearly thirty feet high, and the Champlain Valley got some well-earned national media attention, albeit at Al Roker's expense.

There may not have been snow in New York City, but as you can see, Vermont has plenty to spare.

Photo by Nicole Roscioli

eXtreme Weather eXtra!

Football Flurries / "The Snow Bowl"

Meteorologist Mish Michaels

On the evening of January 19, 2002, a mere three inches of snow blanketed the ground in the Boston metro area. Hardly a record breaker. If the snowstorm had struck a day earlier, or just three hours later, Bostonians would have dusted off their cars, shoveled their driveways, and quickly forgotten the event. But this "minor" storm happened to be nationally televised. Swirls of snow whipped Foxboro stadium helping the New England Patriots defeat the Oakland Raiders on route to the team's first Super Bowl victory. The legacy of what has come to be known as the "Snow Bowl" featured widely publicized pictures of triumphant Patriot player Lonie Paxton making snow angels in the end zone. Those lucky flakes made this otherwise unremarkable storm the most famous three-inch snowfall in New England's history.

Using a leaf blower, crews cleared snow from the field to allow for a game winning kick.

Courtesy of the New England Patriots / David Silverman photo

Adam Vinatieri kicks the winning field goal in the "Snow Bowl Game."

Courtesy of the New England Patriots / David Silverman photo

After a heavy snowfall in Raymond, Maine.

Can you tell which way the wind was blowing?

Photo by Craig Clark

Presidents Day Storm, Feb. 17-18th 2003: It was the biggest blizzard of an already remarkable year for snow storms. Major cities up the east coast were blanketed, including Baltimore, Philadelphia, Washington D.C., and all the way up to New England. Totals on the order of one to three feet were common, some places even more. Boston set a new snowfall total record of 27.5" at Logan Airport, beating the record from the blizzard of '78 as the all-time high snow amount from one storm. This record still stands today.

Central Square in Cambridge, MA in the wake of the President's Day Blizzard of 2003. The plows made it through, but now there's a lot of work to be done with a shovel!

Photo by Sean Graham

Even amazing snowfall totals can't stop the mail in Massachusetts after the President's Day storm of 2003.

Photo by Lin Xu

When even the snowmen are getting sick of snow, you know it is has been a busy year!

Ice storms provide incredible damage and hardships, but can also be amazing to look at.
Photo by Rick Sluben

CHAPTER 2: ICE STORMS

Simply looking at the scenery after an ice storm, you can't help but think how incredibly beautiful it is. Ice completely encases practically everything in sight, turning the entire world shiny and picturesque. When looking at photographs, you can't help but think how pretty it all looks--in fact, breathtaking. As some of the pictures in this chapter show, it's the type of scenery you see on holiday cards. But the other side of these winter storms is the damage and disruption from everyday life they cause.

While they're possible any winter and even multiple times in one season, that doesn't usually happen because a very specific set of circumstances must occur to trigger a severe ice storm. (Phew! Good thing!) The recipe includes very cold air and a healthy amount of freezing rain for an extended time period.

Let's define what freezing rain is: Precipitation that falls from the sky as liquid, but freezes almost instantly upon impact with the ground, trees, or anything else it lands on. This is different from sleet, which is precipitation that falls as frozen ice. Sleet doesn't contribute significantly to ice storms because instead of sticking to accumulated ice, it just bounces off.

Josh's Judgement

You can use this simple test when you're outside to see if you are in sleet or freezing rain: hold out your arm. If it is rain or freezing rain, the drops will either just run down your arm or splash a bit. However, if you see the precipitation bouncing off, as if your arm was a little tiny trampoline, you're seeing sleet! You can also look up into the falling sleet and it will hurt just a little bit as it hits your face.

Freezing rain actually occurs quite a lot in New England winters, but most of the time it either doesn't last long enough to cause major effects, or temperatures warm up enough to stop the icing and even melt it. Storms that have caused the worst damage produced rain for many hours, along with cold temperatures at ground level that were at or below the freezing point of 32 degrees Fahrenheit.

So what occurs in the atmosphere that causes freezing rain, and enough of it for an ice storm danger? Usually, a very cold air mass is over New England before the storm arrives, sometimes after a string of clear but very cold days and nights. This chills everything down below the freezing point. As a winter weather system approaches, it not only brings plenty of precipitation (rain, sleet, snow), but it also usually drags along some warm air from down south.

The warm air moves toward New England, but since cold air is heavier and denser, it remains lodged in place and won't budge. The lighter and less dense warm air is forced to climb up the dome of cold air and moves over us at much higher altitude--meaning that if you were flying an airplane you would actually be flying in warmer air than down below.

So now, when the clouds start to drop either rain or snow, the precipitation falls through this warmer layer of air and melts into rain. When the rain approaches its landing on the

ground, it moves into that very cold air but doesn't have time to freeze before reaching its final landing point. Since that raindrop fell through the sub-freezing air, it is *supercooled*, which basically means it is ready to freeze. As soon as it lands on the frozen ground, a tree, car, road, or anything that is cold, it will instantly turn to ice.

If the freezing rain lasts long enough, then this will continue to happen over and over again. Raindrop after raindrop falls and freezes on everything in sight, and each time, the layer of ice gets a little bit thicker. Before you know it, the ice layers are getting so thick that trees and power lines can't support the weight anymore.

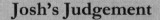

Josh's Judgement

As little as ¼ of an inch of ice is enough to bring down power lines and telephone poles, as it can add up to 500 pounds of weight to each line span.

Ice builds on wires in western Massachusetts.

Photo by Rick Sluben

In the worst of ice storms, so many trees and lines fall that driving a vehicle around can be tricky to nearly impossible. Roads become ice skating rinks and also get blocked by fallen trees, poles and wires. In the days before cars, this wasn't as much of a problem as the animals could still get some footing. But cars need traction and usable roads to get where they're going. Losing your electricity is another of the major life disruptions to deal with. Those who have lost power for as much as one to three weeks in recent ice storms now swear they will always have a generator in storage, just in case.

A generator is brought in to provide power for the Grantham, NH refuge center during the ice storm of December 2008.

Photo courtesy Mike and Kim Hayward, Jr

Ice glistens in front of the Hampstead, NH, meeting house.

Photo by Kristi Schofield

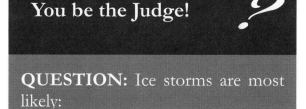

You be the Judge! ?

QUESTION: Ice storms are most likely:

A) In December & January

B) After a thunderstorm

C) When somebody accidentally leaves their freezer door open

ANSWER: A - Ice storms are most likely in December and January.

Notable Ice Storms & Stories

December 29 & 30, 1942: An ice storm of "severe intensity" covered everything with glaze and caused substantial hardships. Worst hit was two-thirds of Massachusetts in areas north and west of Route 495, and a good deal of Vermont (south of Burlington). Also affected: much of interior New Hampshire and northern Connecticut. Damaged trees, telephone poles, and downed wires made transportation very difficult and electric service scarce.

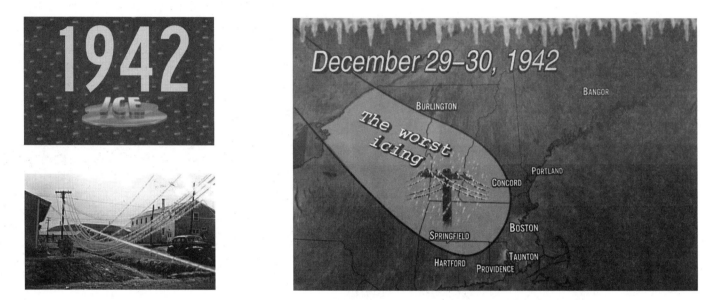

The ice storm of 1942 covered power lines and caused many households
to go without electricity for up to several weeks.

Dec. 16, 1973: This severe ice storm had the greatest effect on Connecticut, Rhode Island, and Western Massachusetts. Between one and three inches of precipitation fell, instantly turning to ice. Eight deaths are attributed to the storm and over 250,000 households lost electricity, including nearly one-third of Connecticut. Some households lost power for a week or more. It was the worst ice storm Connecticut had seen in decades. Telephone poles snapped and trees toppled; in fact, tree damage in the Constitution State was estimated greater than during the Hurricane of 1938.

Hampton, CT- The December 1973 ice storm brought down trees and telephone poles, creating power outages for days and making many roads impassable.

Photo by Harold Hanka

Jan 6, 1994: A severe ice storm hit New England with thousands of trees knocked down and power outages reported. This was a winter season full of ice and snow storms, not only here but throughout much of the eastern United States. The Boston metropolitan area bore some of the worst damage. As is typical of these storms, thousands of electric customers lost service for days.

Ice covered trees in New Hampshire.

Photo by Terri Trier

Jan. 1998: Most of Maine, and big portions of Vermont and New Hampshire (not to mention southern Canada) were crippled in the biggest ice storm in decades. More than half of all residents of Maine lost electricity, some for over two weeks. In an unprecedented move, the state was forced to activate the National Guard, and all sixteen counties of Maine were declared Federal disaster areas. Power crews from as far south as North Carolina came to assist with restoration efforts. (Months later, the state of Maine served them an elaborate lobster dinner to thank them for their efforts.)

An ice-encased tree. *Photo by Jeff Sullivan*

Communications were severely disrupted as thick ice accumulated on transmission towers. Eleven of them failed, including four that totally or partially collapsed. The towers belonged to cellular companies, radio stations, and police, fire, and rescue organizations. At least five radio stations were knocked off the air and two of these stations saw their tower tumble down to the ground: WLNH in Laconia, NH and WEZQ in East Eddington, Maine.

MATT ZIDLE 8

Featured Contributor

The Maine Ice Storm of '98

Meteorologist Matt Zidle, WMTW, Portland, Me

We Mainers are a hardy folk. Living in the far northeast corner of the country, we deal with just about every type of weather. We even experience tornados and hurricanes from time to time. Our summers are usually pleasant, although a heat wave or two can send the temperature and humidity soaring. Our winters are what really sets our weather aside and become the center of conversation.

Many times each winter we are subjected to the wind, rain and snow of the proverbial "nor'easter" or coastal storm. Sometimes large low pressure systems will move to our west and we will get just about every type of precipitation. The worst type of precipitation would have to be freezing rain. To the casual observer it looks like plain old rain falling from the clouds. What soon becomes apparent is that the rain freezes on contact with the ground and other surfaces such as cars, trees, utility poles and wires, etc. The ice storm is perhaps the most awe inspiring of all storms. As glass-like and beautiful as the ice appears, it can have a devastating effect. Such was the case in January of 1998.

On Sunday morning, January 4th, a cold front passed through the state followed by cold, Arctic air. This steady supply of cold air kept the temperatures below freezing. A storm system began moving out of Texas, heading toward western New York. This is usually a fairly typical occurrence leading to a forecast of "snow changing to sleet and freezing rain and eventually all rain" or a "mixed bag of precipitation." There was snow—in fact, nearly a foot of it—in the central and northern part of the state. There was sleet as well and then the freezing rain.

The 1998 ice storm left snow and ice coating everything. Here's a look at Sangerville, Piscataquis County Maine.

Photo copyright Erik M. Stumpfel, 1998. Used with permission

The problem was it never warmed up enough to change that freezing rain over to plain rain away from the coast.

What compounded the problem of the ice was the long duration of the event. A steady supply of moisture kept streaming in over us for days upon days. It wasn't until Saturday, January 10th that the slow-moving storm finally moved into Canada, bringing an end to the freezing rain but not before one to two inches of ice coated everything. The weight of the ice not only brought down tree limbs and power lines, it actually snapped whole utility poles and weighed entire trees to the ground. The devastation was incredible and of massive proportions.

A telephone pole is snapped and rendered useless in Maine after the ice storm of '98.

Photo by T. Berman,
National Weather Service

As if the ice storm alone weren't enough, a cold front passed through the state the following Tuesday, whipping up winds of over 30 mph. The bitter wind caused already weakened trees and power lines and poles to snap. Nearly 80% of the state's population (nearly 1 million people) was left without power, some of whom remained so for nearly two weeks after the storm. In fact, the house across the street from my parents' in Lewiston did not get power restored for almost three weeks. Communication was rendered impossible. Many coastal residents who were spared the destruction of the storm were hit with a subsequent ice storm nearly two weeks later, on Friday, January 23rd. This storm knocked out power to around 75,000 people along the coast.

When I described the storm to friends, some from southern states would compare the devastation to that which is caused by a hurricane. No doubt, hurricanes are the most ferocious of storms; however, they are not followed by such bitterly cold temperatures. The cold temperatures made the cleanup efforts so much harder. People from many states came to Maine to help get us "back on our feet" and local businesses actually donated winter clothing to help them in their efforts.

Maine was not the only state that endured this epic storm. Parts of New Hampshire, Vermont and upstate New York were impacted as well. And the storm would go down in the record books as the most devastating weather event ever across southern Quebec, including the densely populated Montreal area. No doubt, there have been and will be more ice storms, but hopefully never so destructive and paralyzing as the "Ice Storm of 1998."

Looks like the game has hit a little snag.

Photo by Ryan Breton

The Tale of The Tumbling Transmitter Tower!

Laconia, NH: As remembered by Peter Stohrer and Joe Collie

PETER: As a contract radio engineer, I can get calls from radio stations at any time. On this particular day my phone rang early in the evening and the voice on the other end, in hurried words, said, "WLNH and WBHG are off the air." On the way there, I mused ,"Most likely the persistent icing that had continued throughout the day somehow is behind it all." Little did I realize.

When I arrived at the studios I was met by a young Joe Collie, who was finishing up his on-air shift. We rushed to the tower site to find out what the situation was. Leaving the studios we began to gain elevation going up Parade Road and in less than a mile the landscape was transformed to a glistening world of ice. It became apparent that power was out, which would account for the stations being off the air.

As we crept cautiously into the transmitter site, it was clear the station was in trouble. Looking up at the tower through the freezing rain and admiring the beauty of its newly donned ice jacket, we noticed that the tower was no longer perpendicular to the earth but had a definite curve due to the weight of ice. From the view at the base of the tower the top section at 300 feet was arced with an overhang of about 10 feet. The tower was coated in ice and the freezing rain was still falling!

JOE: I remember the ice being about 2 inches thick all the way around the tower. We needed to provide power to transmitter, so we ran jumper cables to it from the station van which was parked next to the entrance. The jumper cables came in the door and down the hall to the engineering room. Running a station off power from the van was wild!

PETER: The next morning dawned beautiful. As we made our way back to the transmitter site, the sunlight shining through the ice took our breath away. As I crested the hill where normally the tower came into view, the skyline was empty and the tower was gone. After pulling into the parking area, we saw, as we feared, the tower had collapsed.

JOE: When the sun came out that morning, it melted the eastern side of the tower first. Since the weight was so uneven at this point, the tower came down. The tower crash was very significant, because WLNH is a primary Emergency Alert Station in New Hampshire, and fourteen other stations rely on it for information.

Initially, we borrowed another station's remote van to mount an antenna on their mast, giving us some height. That didn't work, so one of the station's engineers suggested we erect two of the fallen tower sections and put antennas on them (one for each station). This worked and we had two towers, each one 25-30 feet high. The two stations, both normally 6,000 watts, ran at approximately 1,000 watts with very low towers, until the new tower was erected. Because this happened in winter, we had to wait for good weather for the tower crew. The new stick went online and we were back at full power April 15, 1998 - more than three months after the collapse.

The WLNH Radio tower lies on the ground after collapsing from the weight of the ice.

Photos by Richard Wholey

Fear of Frozen Fish

By Steve Dillard – Westbrook, Maine

After the ice storm, we lost power for five days. I had a 50-gallon tropical aquarium and was worried about all the expensive fish freezing to death. The pet shop told me to just throw blankets over it and hope for the best. When the power came back on and I took the blankets off, the fish were all in some kind of suspended animation. Some were upside down in the plants, some floating, etc. When it started circulating and warming up, all the fish (about a dozen) came back to life and only one died. I was amazed.

2008 December Ice Storm: A memorable ice event that was the worst in a decade for many parts of the region. Its most disastrous effects were in New Hampshire, central Massachusetts and southern Maine. The primary damage was due to downed trees and telephone poles. This storm is blamed for two deaths in New England. Hundreds of thousands of people lost power for days and even weeks; at its peak, over a million New Englanders were in the dark. One common memory people have from the storm is from the middle of the night, when enough ice accumulated on trees and they began to fall. Ask

The devastation can sometimes be forgotten when you're looking at the beauty of the ice.

Photo Terri Trier

nearly anyone in the affected area and they'll tell you all about the loud cracks of the trees falling, which sounded like gun shots, explosions, or thunder.

A shirt, made for charity, sold after the ice storm of 2008 to those who "survived" the ice.

Ice-covered trees come crashing down, blocking the road in Hampstead, NH

A road in Marlboro, VT is turned into a skating rink and obstacle course.

Photo by Richard Cogliano,
Vermont Emergency Management

Trees down in East Derry, NH. Most people who lived through the ice storm of 2008 reported hearing hundreds of "gunshot" sounds, which were actually trees falling in the night. *Photo by Trista Kort*

An ice and snow world in Sunapee, NH. For the time being, crews cut trees up and left them on the side of the road to be disposed of later. *Photo courtesy Mike and Kim Hayward, Jr.*

Featured Contributor

Mike Haddad

Ice Storm December 11-12, 2008

Meteorologist Mike Haddad – WMUR-TV, New Hampshire

There it was—low pressure moving up from the south with lots of moisture. (Our computer guidance was forecasting rainfall amounts that we normally get in a three week period, to fall in just a 36-hour period.) There it also was—plenty of cold air at the surface. Now in most cases, that means snow. The trouble this time around: a mild layer of air above the cold surface. This now had the makings of an impressive ice storm.

The National Weather Service posted ice storm warnings well in advance of the event. One thing was for certain: there would be some significant ice buildup. What wasn't so certain was the extreme impact the ice would have. From a forecasting standpoint, I don't think anyone imagined that over 400,000 electric customers in New Hampshire alone would lose power!

So, the rain fell, and the ice built up as temperatures stayed just below freezing. More rain fell, and more ice built up. By the time evening fell, over a half inch of ice had accumulated on trees and power lines. Several hours later, the power outages began. I recall leaving after the 11 PM news the night of Thursday, December 11th. Power was already out to over fifty thousand customers. I remember thinking that the number could grow to 100,000 or 125,000; certainly not the incredible number that actually occurred.

As one might expect, it was a struggle for utility companies to restore power to everyone quickly. Some residents remained without power for over two weeks. States of emergencies were declared and schools were closed for several days, and in some cases a few weeks! Property damage was measured in the hundreds of millions.

A few carbon monoxide poisoning deaths occurred in the region due to the running of gas powered generators indoors. Carbon monoxide is a colorless and odorless gas that can kill. This should serve as a reminder to be extra careful if

Ice covers all the landscaping in a New Hampshire home after the December 2008 storm.

Photo by Jeff Sullivan

you plan to run a generator in the future. Be sure to always run one outdoors and well away from the home.

There was a noticeable difference between the ice storm of 1998 and the December 2008 storm, in addition to the regions they affected. That was the intensity in which the rain fell. In 1998, freezing rain occurred, but it was mostly light in intensity. The problem was the duration of the freezing rain, which was two and a half to three days, resulting in widespread damage to northern New England and southeast Canada. This time around, the freezing rain fell at a moderate to heavy clip for a much shorter time. The results from both storms, however, were the same: tremendous devastation.

Ice storms are very difficult to predict, especially since they don't happen that often to the degree of the 1998 and 2008 ones. What we do know is that extreme ice storms have occurred before, as evidenced above. What we do not know is when the next one will happen. It could be next year, or twenty years from now. In any event, you should always be prepared for any kind of weather from late fall through early spring in New England, including lots of ice.

Paralyzed Without Power

By Kathe Cussen – East Hampstead, NH

We learned two important truths during the Ice Storm of 2008: the generosity of neighbors and friends with generators made life without electricity a lot more bearable, and we rapidly became creative experimenters when forced to cook all meals on a wood stove and function in temperatures below 50°F.

Every day, we woke up hopeful that it would be THE day we would have electricity restored. Days on end having to go to work without a shower or a hot meal, and sleeping on the floor in front of the woodstove, were taking their toll on our sanity!

On Christmas Eve, 13 days after losing power, the lights went on resulting in the best Christmas ever!

Photo by Rick Sluben

December 2008 Ice Storm in Western Massachusetts

Meteorologist Rick Sluben – WWLP TV 22, Springfield, Ma

Western Massachusetts. It's a rather pleasant parcel of land stretching from the waters of the pristine Quabbin reservoir and its "accidental wilderness" to the beautiful, weather-worn Berkshire Hills. It includes of course the culturally and agriculturally rich Pioneer Valley, split by the magnificent but sometimes malicious Connecticut River. It's a small geographical area with just four counties but packs in some diverse topography which can mean some formidable forecast "challenges!"

One of the more memorable challenges in my near-decade of tracking storms out here was in mid-December of 2008. December 11-12th of that year will forever be known as the Great Central New England Ice Storm. A slow-moving, soaking rainstorm moved up the Appalachians along a stalled out front on December 10th and then right over New England on the 11th and 12th. Cold, Arctic air parked just to our north was pulled in as the storm emptied itself on us and the over-running (warm air riding up over cold air) was on! My forecasts for all rain in the valley but "ice storm conditions" in the hill towns with widespread power outages were realized, but no one anticipated the level of destruction that followed in the hills. The rain fell heavily in the Pioneer Valley with a storm total of three-five inches. In the higher elevations it was freezing rain—heavy at times!

Just after the storm ended and I finished my shift, I grabbed my camera and drove up into the hills to see the devastation first-hand. My drive took me climbing into the Quabbin hills on Route 202 through Belchertown and then to Pelham and Shutesbury. According to my GPS, at precisely 800 feet the landscape changed from ice-free to a foreign, frozen spectacle in a snap. Ice accretion of ½"-1 inch bent and snapped so many trees that, if it weren't for the glaze on top, the scene would pass for tornado damage. Two distinct sounds filled the air—the first being gunshot-like cracks from tree limbs splintering and crashing down, spraying the ground with ice shrapnel, and the other the hum of distant generators from residents suddenly thrown into the Stone Age and quite literally a powerless situation. More than one million central New England residents lost power in the storm, some not to see it restored for weeks!

As I left the area to return home, something amazing happened: the sun came out. (See my picture at the beginning of this chapter.) The storm clouds cleared and the sky became the most beautiful blue you'd ever see. The photographer in me grinned widely. What a show! The late-day sun through the icy chandeliers showed Mother Nature's beauty after her fury. Yes indeed, she can be both a beauty and a beast.

RIGHT AND BELOW: *Photos by Rick Sluben*

BOTTOM: The beauty of the ice and sunset over Northfield, NH.

Photo courtesy Holly Parker

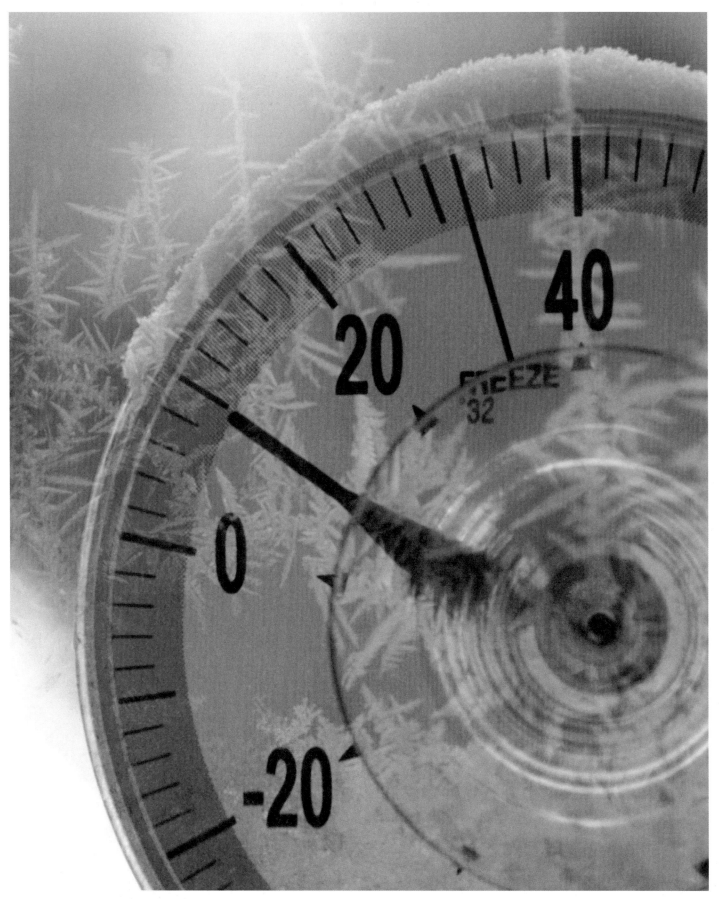

When temperatures drop to sub-freezing levels, it changes life for a while.
Photo by Judy Knesel, Awakenings Blog

CHAPTER 3: COLD SPELLS

If you live in New England, one thing you're certain to deal with every winter is cold weather. There's really no way you can avoid it in this part of the country. Each winter season is different, and some are warmer than others. But most winters have many cold waves and at least one to three *arctic outbreaks*, meaning the coldest weather spells of the year. Add in some gusty wind, and you've got the type of weather that keeps most people indoors huddled up next to the fire or other heat source. Plenty of hardy New Englanders, however, do brave the cold and go out to face the chill head on, but they do so wrapped up in many layers of warm clothing.

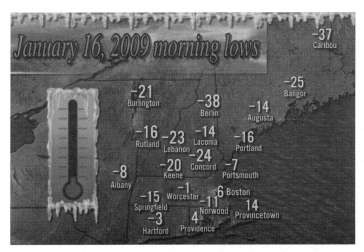

Arctic air masses begin up to our north, usually somewhere over Canada or sometimes even the frozen Arctic Ocean. The air sits over the very cold land or ice and gets colder and colder, as there is very little or no sunlight up there in winter. Then a weather system moves in and pushes this frigid air down toward us. As it approaches, it usually warms a little bit (meteorologists say that it *modifies*) while traveling south, but still brings extremely cold temperatures. Because these air masses are often quite large, they can bring several cold days and icy nights before moving out.

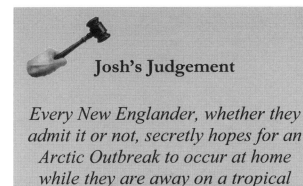

Josh's Judgement

Every New Englander, whether they admit it or not, secretly hopes for an Arctic Outbreak to occur at home while they are away on a tropical vacation.

ARCTIC AIR GATHERS IN CANADA

Wind makes it worse

Wind can make a cold day into a terribly cold *feeling* day. Just walking across the parking lot to get to your car or destination can be brutal. Why does the wind make it feel so much colder? It's because of the *Wind Chill Factor*, which is a very interesting phenomenon.

Our bodies generate heat. It surrounds us to keep us warmer. This is why we dress up in heavy outdoor gear or put blankets over us to stay warm, because they trap our body warmth. You may not always notice this heat surrounding you, but you sure do notice it when the wind blows it away! That's exactly what happens. As your body produces heat, the wind blows it away from you so it feels even colder to you. It's sort of like nature's way of turning off your body's heating system. This is why your parents (and even we weathercasters on TV) always told you to dress in layers and cover all exposed skin when going out in this type of weather. Dressing in layers keeps your body heat with you, and with everything covered up, much less warmth gets blown away since it's trapped.

Because of this reason, only warm-blooded living things can be affected by the wind chill factor. If your car is parked outside in windy conditions, it doesn't react any differently than it would if there were no wind.

Josh's Judgement

So here's the age old question I get asked all the time: If water is put outside with a temperature of 37 degrees, but the wind chill factor is below the freezing mark, will the water freeze? Since you've read this far, you probably already know that the answer is no. Interestingly enough, studies have shown that if you put a bucket of water outside to freeze (when it's below 32° Fahrenheit), it actually can freeze slightly faster when it's windy! Why? Because as the water cools down, warmer air rises away from it, and the wind moves this warmth away faster, allowing it to cool off a little bit more quickly.

This is also the case with falling precipitation. Even if the wind chill factor is below 32°, snow can still melt into rain if the actual temperature is above 32°.

NWS Windchill Chart

Wind (mph)	Temperature (°F)																	
Calm	40	35	30	25	20	15	10	5	0	-5	-10	-15	-20	-25	-30	-35	-40	-45
5	36	31	25	19	13	7	1	-5	-11	-16	-22	-28	-34	-40	-46	-52	-57	-63
10	34	27	21	15	9	3	-4	-10	-16	-22	-28	-35	-41	-47	-53	-59	-66	-72
15	32	25	19	13	6	0	-7	-13	-19	-26	-32	-39	-45	-51	-58	-64	-71	-77
20	30	24	17	11	4	-2	-9	-15	-22	-29	-35	-42	-48	-55	-61	-68	-74	-81
25	29	23	16	9	3	-4	-11	-17	-24	-31	-37	-44	-51	-58	-64	-71	-78	-84
30	28	22	15	8	1	-5	-12	-19	-26	-33	-39	-46	-53	-60	-67	-73	-80	-87
35	28	21	14	7	0	-7	-14	-21	-27	-34	-41	-48	-55	-62	-69	-76	-82	-89
40	27	20	13	6	-1	-8	-15	-22	-29	-36	-43	-50	-57	-64	-71	-78	-84	-91
45	26	19	12	5	-2	-9	-16	-23	-30	-37	-44	-51	-58	-65	-72	-79	-86	-93
50	26	19	12	4	-3	-10	-17	-24	-31	-38	-45	-52	-60	-67	-74	-81	-88	-95
55	25	18	11	4	-3	-11	-18	-25	-32	-39	-46	-54	-61	-68	-75	-82	-89	-97
60	25	17	10	3	-4	-11	-19	-26	-33	-40	-48	-55	-62	-69	-76	-84	-91	-98

Frostbite Times [ ] 30 minutes [ ] 10 minutes [ ] 5 minutes

Produced by the National Weather Service, this chart shows how cold it *feels* with specific temperatures and wind speeds. Read the temperature on the top and the wind speed on the left, and where they meet you'll find the estimated wind chill factor.

When the wind chill factor hits extreme low temperatures, it gets downright dangerous. Generally, if you're outside for extended periods of time, frostbite starts to become a possibility when the wind chill factor gets to or below -20° Fahrenheit. The chart shows how long it may take for each temperature and wind speed.

You be the Judge!

QUESTION: When the temperature dips to near -20° F, if you throw a cup of boiling water into the air, it will:

A) Instantly vaporize

B) Instantly become a block of ice

C) Instantly turn into ice coffee

ANSWER: A - It vaporizes!

Interesting Cold Weather Facts

•If you ever see -40° on a thermometer, you can call it either Fahrenheit or Celsius. This is where the two temperature scales meet. Of course, if it's -40°, you've got much more important things on your mind than interesting factoids—like getting warm!

•Even when the temperature is below 32°F, snow and ice can still melt with enough direct sunshine. Sunlight can warm individual items up above the melting point even if the air is not.

•Almost every time New England has an arctic outbreak, the cold air came here from Canada. (Thanks, Canada!)

•Although the freezing point of water is 32° Fahrenheit, if you add salt, the freezing point is lowered. This is why salt is added to roads and driveways, to melt snow and ice.

Dangers of extreme cold

When cold and wind bring temperatures down to these levels, it is serious business. Schools move recess inside and many outdoor activities are rescheduled. Outdoor workers need to take frequent breaks to warm up indoors, and many people just cancel recreational activities to stay in the warmth. The risk of frostbite or even *hypothermia* is just too high and the consequences too severe.

The signs of hypothermia
(Hypo=less + thermia=temperature)
When conditions lower our core body temperature below 95°F, we go into hypothermia. If not treated, hypothermia can result in death. Here are some signs that hypothermia may be occurring:
Uncontrollable shivering (It goes away as body temperature gets dangerously low.)
Weakness, loss of coordination
Confusion, poor judgment
Blueness of skin
Stumbling, slow movement
Trouble speaking
Drowsiness / apathy
Rapid heart rate (Initially, then it slows as body temperature gets dangerously low.)

Arctic outbreaks also cost money. First off, your furnace or woodstove works much harder to keep the house warm, which means more fuel. Secondly, businesses suffer because people stay home. Oddly enough, much of the time, the coldest and windiest weather is also accompanied by sunny skies, so it looks often looks like a beautiful day out the window. The low sun angle and a very cold air mass can render the sun rather ineffective in spreading warmth.

Cold weather can cause damage to property as well. Frost heaves and potholes form in the roads, needing to be fixed in the spring. Pipes freeze and burst, which can also cause major damage to houses and businesses. Some cars won't even start in extreme cold.

A frost has formed after a night in New Hampshire.

Photo by Terri Trier

You be the Judge! ?

QUESTION: The winter of 1848 was so cold that:

A) Niagara Falls froze completely

B) A glacier formed in Providence, RI

C) Politicians actually kept their hands in their *own* pockets!

ANSWER: A - Quite often Niagara Falls freezes on top, but this particular winter the water flow stopped completely for a short time.

There is no doubt, arctic outbreaks can have drastic effects on life and how we live it. Being prepared with proper clothing and other supplies can make a big difference in how well you manage. Don't forget your pets during cold weather, too—let them stay indoors. Oh yeah, here's a special tip of the hat to those who have to work outside in these types of conditions.

All-time coldest temperatures for several New England cities:		
-41°	Caribou, ME	February 1955
-41°	Berlin, NH	December 1933
-39°	Portland, ME	February 1943
-37°	Concord, NH	January 1984
-38°	Springfield, VT	January 1957
-33°	Augusta, ME	January 1975
-30°	Boston, MA	January 1946
-30°	Burlington, VT	January 1957
-24°	New Haven, CT	February 1943
-24°	Worcester, MA	February 1943
-24°	Laconia, NH	January 1994
-24°	Hartford, CT	February 1943
-18°	Springfield, MA	January 1984
-17°	Providence, RI	February 1934
-8°	New Haven, MA	January 1957
-6°	Chatham, MA	January 2004
-4°	Provincetown, MA	January 2004

03/23/2010 08:20

Looks like this cat knows where to stay when the weather turns cold.

Photo courtesy Ulocal.wmur.com Ulocal

Notable Cold Weather Stories

February 1979: Imagine a 13-day stretch of weather when the *high* temperature for the day doesn't go above 10° Fahrenheit. On seven of those 13 days, the high for the day doesn't even go above zero! Nope, we're not talking about somewhere up in the arctic. I'm describing Burlington, Vermont, between February 6th and 18th, 1979. This was after a week of temperatures topping off in the teens, warm compared to the nearly two weeks that were on the way. Other cities around New England were also frigid during that period, but the Burlington stats are simply unbelievable. Here are the actual high temperatures during that stretch of almost two weeks. Remember, these are the *high* temperatures, this is where the temperature PEAKED!

Feb 6	7°	Feb 11	-7°	Feb 16	0°
Feb 7	10°	Feb 12	3°	Feb 17	-4°
Feb 8	10°	Feb 13	-2°	Feb 18	5°
Feb 9	9°	Feb 14	-2°		
Feb 10	-5°	Feb 15	0°		

The next day, this super cold wave broke, with temperatures reaching a "balmy" 21°. Wow, glad things warmed up so much!

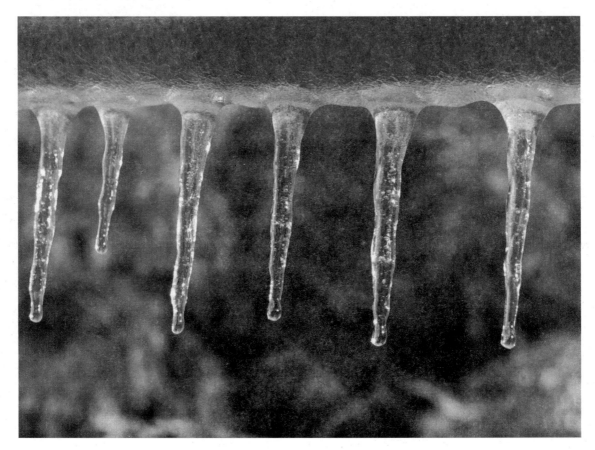

Photo courtesy Ulocal.wmur.com ⒰**local**

January 2004 Cold Wave: Much of the month was dominated by unusually cold weather in New England. Boston had one of its coldest winters on record and most of the region froze for weeks at a time. Here are some of the highlights (or are they lowlights?) and cold nights from the month of January 2004:

City	# times in single digits	# times below zero	Coldest night of the month
Caribou, ME	27	20	-22
Whitefield, NH	26	17	-36
Houlton, ME	26	19	-25
Burlington, VT	24	14	-20
Bangor, ME	20	14	-15
Concord, NH	20	11	-13
Portland, ME	18	11	-11
Worcester, MA	18	8	-12
Springfield, MA	17	7	-9
Hartford, CT	15	3	-4
Providence, RI	10	3	-6

eXtreme Weather eXtra!

The Year Without a Summer: Although it wasn't an "arctic outbreak," this story is worthy of mention because of the unusual cold New England felt during the summer of 1816. At the time, the year was also referred to as, "Eighteen hundred and froze to death." There was snow in June! Residents of Vermont, New Hampshire, and Maine all had to find their shovels as 5-10 inches of snow and sleet accumulated (more in places like Danville, VT). Even southern New England states reported snow falling, but not accumulating, that June day. During many nights in July, August, and September there was frost and temperatures dipping below the freezing point. New Englanders woke up to ice as thick as glass in all six states every month of the summer. Many farmers lost their crops due to the cold and frost, lack of sunlight to ripen produce, and drought conditions.

Most scientific explanations put the blame on the volcanic eruption of Mount Tambora on the island of Sumbawa, Indonesia in 1815. Dust from the volcano rose all the way up to the stratosphere and took a year to be blown around the Earth to North America. Since it filled the atmosphere and blocked incoming sunlight, it limited warmth during an already cool summer.

As a side note, many fed-up farmers moved away from New England after these events, and this began the movement of big farming to the middle portions of the country.

Photo courtesy Ulocal.wmur.com

Bitter cold, dense fog, heavy snow, and record wind... 6,288-foot Mount Washington is home of the world's worst weather!

CHAPTER 4: MOUNT WASHINGTON

Written by the staff of the Mount Washington Observatory

On April 12, 1934, on the rocky, desolate mountaintop of Mount Washington, a storm raged furiously. The frenzied wind pummeled the summit and at 1:21 PM, a gust of 231 mph was recorded, setting a new world record that lasted for more than 60 years. We know this thanks to a small group of dedicated individuals, who in 1932 formed a non-profit scientific organization called the Mount Washington Observatory. Their mission was easy: to observe and document the extreme weather on the summit of Mount Washington. As simple as this mission may seem, in reality it is far from simple when temperatures are well below 0°F, winds are howling over hurricane force, and the thick fog and blowing snow create white-out conditions. And that is just a "normal" mid-winter day on Mount Washington! The aforementioned fog (present over 60% of the year), along with the cold temperatures, creates a phenomenon called rime ice, which is literally frozen fog. The tiny unfrozen water droplets that make up the fog freeze upon impact with any surface they touch—including the buildings, rocks, instruments,

Here's why people associated with Mount Washington lovingly refer to it as "the rock pile."

and even beards, eye-lashes, clothing, or an animal's fur. These challenging weather conditions require that the Observatory's weather station on the summit of Mount Washington still be staffed year-round, despite significant advances in automated instrumentation in the last 10 to 20 years. In fact, an observer physically goes outside, once per hour, 24 hours per day, 365 days per year to do their observations. This dedication to observing Mount Washington's weather has produced a detailed, nearly uninterrupted climate record spanning almost 80 years.

Let's take a look at some of the extremes and highlights within that impressive climate record. The lowest temperature ever recorded by the Observatory is a bone-chilling -46.5°F while the highest recorded temperature is only 72°F. As far as precipitation goes, 1969 holds the record for most liquid precipitation and snowfall, with 130.14 inches and 566.4 inches respectively. Compare that to an average year, which sees about 315 inches of snowfall and 101.91 inches of liquid. During the "winter" months of October through May, a wind gust exceeding hurricane force is measured every other day on average, while a wind gust exceeding

Highest temperature ever recorded: 72° F

Lowest temperature ever recorded: -46.5° F

100 mph is measured 1 out of every 4 days on average. Sub-freezing temperatures and snowfall have been measured in every month of the year, as well as wind speeds well in excess of 100 mph. Saving the best for last, the previously mentioned 231 mph wind gust still stands to this day as the highest wind speed recorded anywhere in the Northern and Western Hemispheres, and the fastest wind ever observed by man.

Checking the anemometer for ice. It must stay clean so that it can measure wind speed.

Although Mount Washington is the tallest peak in the northeastern United States at 6,288 feet, on a global scale it is really quite insignificant. Also, at just shy of 45 degrees North latitude, there are certainly mountains as big or bigger that are significantly farther north. Given all this, why is it that such extreme weather conditions exist here, especially when it comes to the wind? There are a lot of factors that must be taken into consideration while discussing the answer to this question, like geography, weather patterns, and how the air interacts with the terrain.

New England is often referred to as the "tailpipe of the United States" because almost every storm system that traverses the country is steered towards the northeast. When the storm tracks are averaged over time, New Hampshire's White Mountains sit right in the path of three of the major storm routes: storms that come up the coast (nor'easters), storms that come across from Canada along the St. Lawrence River valley, and storms that come from the Mississippi and Ohio River valleys. This translates to frequent storms passing through New England, often at the strongest point in their life cycle.

So that's how the weather gets to Mount Washington, but it's the way that the air then interacts with the terrain that makes the weather so severe, especially when it comes to the wind. As the tallest mountain in the northeast, there is nothing to inhibit the wind for thousands of miles around. This exposure, coupled with the prominence of the mountain, acts to accelerate the wind. The prevailing wind directions for Mount Washington are west and northwest, which happen to be exactly perpendicular to the orientation of the Presidential Range, of which Mount Washington is a part. Additionally, Mount Washington rises over 4,000 vertical feet above the valley floors on either side. The acceleration occurs when air is forced up and over the summit and is essentially "squeezed" between the top of the mountain and more stable layers in the atmosphere above. We call this the "garden-hose effect." If you've ever put your thumb over the end of an open garden hose and made the opening smaller, you know that the water will come out of the end of the hose faster as you make the hole smaller. The same physical principal, the Bernoulli Effect, also happens on Mount Washington. As we've already briefly discussed, the wind is just one variable that makes the weather so extreme on Mount Washington. What about the rest?

The reason for the incredible amount of fog, as well as a good chunk of the precipitation that falls each year, can be attributed to moist air being lifted up the mountainside through a process called orographic lifting. As air rises up the slopes of Mount Washington, it is cooled. If the air mass is moist enough, it will likely cool to its dew point before the air starts descending on the other side of the mountain. When the air cools to its dew point, it will form fog or sometimes even precipitation. There are some days when the valley below is experiencing a bright sunny day while the summit is encased in a cloud with heavy snowfall, all thanks to orographic lifting.

Let's not forget about those bitterly cold temperatures. As was already mentioned, air cools as it rises. Because of this property of the atmosphere, the summit of Mount Washington typically runs about 20 to 30 degrees colder than the surrounding valleys. During transition seasons, this temperature difference can be even more drastic. For instance, there can be some fall or spring days that are in the 60s or even 70s with bright sunshine in the valley, while at the summit the temperature is below freezing with fog and snow.

In the end, it isn't just one of these variables on its own that earns Mount Washington the reputation for having the "World's Worst Weather." It is the combination of extreme elements that creates the truly unique and intense weather conditions found here, high atop the windswept summit of Mount Washington.

Life and Work

Six full-time staff and one cat call the Mount Washington Observatory home on a regular basis. There are two crews, each with three weather observers that work alternating, week-long shifts on the mountain. Each observer, in addition to being certified by the National Weather

ABOVE: A simply breathtaking view of the clouds down below the mountain. They almost look like you could walk on them.

RIGHT: On the observatory deck, everything is completely covered in snow and rime ice for a large part of the year.

RIGHT: As wind travels up and down the mountains, it creates amazing patterns in the clouds.

BELOW: Sunrises and sunsets take on new meaning on top of the mountain.

Thank you to the Mount Washington Observatory for all the photographs in this chapter.

Service to take weather observations, has a very specific focus. Each crew comprises one meteorology specialist, one education specialist and one information technology specialist.

The meteorology specialist is also known as the "night observer." This brave soul works while the rest of the world sleeps, and is responsible for quality checking the day's observations as well as keeping all the weather documents and records up to date. As a degreed meteorologist, they do a large portion of the forecasting that is published to our website, *www.MountWashington.org*. Their voices can also be heard on radio stations throughout New England, as well as New Hampshire Public Radio.

Snow and wind can quickly reduce visibility down to zero in a hurry. Now you know why they dress so snugly just to go outside.

With the advancement of technology, and the integration of that technology into the meteorological field, the Mount Washington Observatory has become increasingly dependent upon computers, servers, data-loggers and other high-tech equipment. Today's Observatory requires staff who can write computer programs, fix broken instruments, and improve our data collection methods. The information technology specialist position requires an incredibly diverse and unique skill set. Not only do they need to be proficient in C++, PHP, and LabView programming languages, they also need to learn METAR weather observation coding standards and basic mountain weather forecasting methods.

The final of the three observer positions, the education specialist, is on the summit to help fulfill the educational part of the Observatory's mission. The mountain's incredible weather and international acclaim has made the Observatory a tremendous resource for weather, climate and general science education. The education specialist helps to connect students, visitors and program participants with the awe and wonder of Mount Washington. We do this through a variety of programs, including weather station tours, on-site day and overnight programs, through our comprehensive website and also through our newest endeavor, conducting videoconferencing programs with schools across the nation and around the world.

And we would be remiss if we were to leave out one of the most important members of our summit crew. Ever since the Observatory's inception in 1932, it has been home to at least one cat. "Marty" is the latest in a long line of mountaintop felines, reigning at the summit since January of 2008. He thoroughly believes he is the king of the mountain and, really, who are we to argue? He's up here more than anyone else, and certainly gets more attention than anyone else!

Living on top of a mountain for a week at a time, especially one that produces the kind of weather that this one does, can lead to some very interesting experiences for the observers.

For example: thunderstorms. Although the weather during the summer months is, on the whole, considerably tamer than during the winter, there are moments of excitement, and thunderstorms never fail to produce these moments. Thunder is created by lightning, super-heating and expanding the air through which it travels; the thunder is the resulting sound from the air rapidly cooling and contracting. And the sound that thunder produces is incredibly loud on Mount Washington. Despite this startling and often frightening characteristic of thunder, when it comes to thunderstorms, lightning is where the real danger lies.

Everyone knows that lightning, though majestic and enchanting, is dangerous, especially on the tallest mountain in the region. It is dangerous enough that it's one of only two situations when observers will not venture out to retrieve the precipitation can, which is situated in the middle of the summit and is made of metal. Because of Mount Washington's elevation, there are a lot of tall radio transmission towers on the summit that attract lightning strikes like giant lightning rods. And as thunderstorms approach, the air will sometime literally crackle with static electricity before the summit and its buildings are hit by lightning. As long as observers stay inside, the dangers that come with thunderstorms are kept to a minimum.

The only other time observers will not retrieve the precipitation can is when winds are too strong to be able to safely walk outside. The precipitation can is 34" tall and 8" round, and can be rather cumbersome, especially in strong, gusty winds. If an observer accidentally tilts the opening into the wind, it acts like a sail and will either fly out of the observer's hands or take them with it. The threshold for when a wind is considered too strong is different for everyone, and wind direction is also taken into consideration. Generally speaking though, when winds become sustained over 100 mph, observer safety usually outweighs the retrieval of the precipitation can.

Another interesting task that any observer becomes familiar with very quickly on the mountain is de-icing. Before talking about the actual act of de-icing, let's focus on the reason that observers have to do it in the first place: rime ice. As you may recall from earlier in this chapter, rime ice is literally frozen fog. Freezing fog, which is simply a cloud in contact with the surface of the earth, consists of tiny water droplets at a temperature below freezing – but they have not frozen yet. These droplets, which are said to be super-cooled, are extremely unstable and will freeze instantaneously as they come in contact with a solid surface. This can lead to the development of long, brittle, feathery fingers of ice that enshroud every summit building in a brilliant white coating, giving the summit its distinctive wintertime mystique. Although the appearance of these ice structures, which can grow to several feet in length, is quite astounding, they can wreak havoc on weather instruments attempting to gather accurate data, especially when it comes to anemometers, devices used to measure the speed of the wind.

There are several varieties of anemometers utilized to measure the winds that have given Mount Washington its sinister reputation, but the primary and most unique device is the pitot-static anemometer. A pitot tube is conventionally used on an airplane to determine the speed of the aircraft. However, the Observatory staff of the past took this concept and flipped it—attaching the pitot tube to a wind vane and installing it on the top of the tower to measure the speed at which the air is moving. One of the most critical characteristics of the pitot-static anemometer is its ability to be heated to temperatures hot enough to burn a human hand. Even though the pitot is heated, rime ice can still develop on certain parts of the instrument, along with the instruments that are not heated. It then becomes the job of the brave Mount Washington weather observers to venture to the top of the tower and eliminate this ice.

"De-icing" is a task that is commonly done during each hourly observation when the summit is ensconced in freezing fog, but sometimes it must be done with increased frequency during particularly severe icing events. De-icing encompasses a climb to the very top of the tower, the location on the summit exposed to the full brunt of the elements, "gently" wielding a crow bar and removing ice from any instrument collecting it.

When the fog finally fades away, the snow ceases, and the violent winds subside, many feet of snow can be left behind, usually rationed into large drifts around the summit, with a thick coating of rime ice acting as icing on the cake. It's at this point when the seemingly endless task of digging out commences! Despite the technological developments in the spirit of snow blowers that have aided snow removal procedures in locations nearer to sea level, gusty winds that pack the snow very densely render many of those technologies completely ineffective. However, that is not to say shoveling is completely foolproof—with strong gusty winds and light fluffy flakes for fodder, hours of arduous shoveling can be undone within a matter of minutes. Snowdrifts in excess of 20 feet are all too common during the bleak winter months and are constantly shifting around the summit with the altering wind directions.

A common question we field, especially in the winter, is: how do you get up and down the mountain? Regardless of the time of year, options for access to the summit of Mount Washington are fairly limited, but this is especially true during the winter months. As one can imagine, Observatory staff have one of the most unique commutes on the planet, and no two commutes are identical, thanks to erratic and occasionally brutal weather conditions. During the winter, the Observatory crew loads into a 10-person passenger cab that is mounted on the back of a Bombardier snow tractor. The snow tractor is a vehicle one would normally see grooming the slopes of a ski resort—a good fit for climbing the side of a 6,288-foot mountain. Snow tractor trips to the summit can be as brief as one hour in the best of weather, but as lengthy as five hours, with the latter resulting from thick freezing fog and blinding blowing snow tossed about by hurricane force winds. While the winter commute is generally not too treacherous on the bottom half of the Auto Road which lies below tree line, it can turn perilous in a hurry once the Bombardier emerges from the forest and begins its ascent above tree line.

The "Five-Mile" segment of the Mount Washington Auto Road is literally carved into the side of the mountain, with a sheer drop on the opposing side. Despite the skill of seasoned snow tractor operators, visibility below fifty feet along with wind gusts in excess of 100 mph are enough to shake even the most stoic individual. Just above this Five-Mile stretch is a section of the Auto Road known as "Cragway," which is infamous for its colossal snow drifts, massive enough to bring even the most formidable snow tractor to a halt. It is here where many trips to the summit are forced to turn back.

While snow tractors are excellent when snow is packed and deep, they struggle greatly with the slushy and slippery conditions that are prevalent in the transition seasons and are often unnecessary altogether once the snow begins to melt off the road. It is during these times of year that the Observatory staff utilizes a 4-wheel drive van coupled with chains on the tires for added traction. Once summer begins to show itself, and the Auto Road is completely clear of snow and ice, the chains come off, and the trip becomes much less treacherous and lengthy, lasting a scant thirty minutes or so in the Observatory van.

The ultimate destination of these adventures is a concrete structure that sits atop the summit, Mt. Washington State Park's Sherman Adams Visitor Center. The Observatory's iconic tower, world-famous weather station, and modest living quarters, can all be found here. The lower level of the facility houses our kitchen, living room, and five bunkrooms that can accommodate as many as seventeen individuals. Because the staff works and lives on the summit for a week at a time, this space acts as a second home for its inhabitants. The hub of activity, our "weather room," can be found on the

Instruments must be cleaned hourly so that they continue working properly.

main level of the facility, along with other offices and work spaces. The Observatory's 30-foot tower sits on the western end of the building and accommodates our wind-measuring devices, or anemometers, that are used by observers to obtain real-time wind data.

Believe it or not, the ferocity of Mount Washington can and will occasionally abate, treating the staff to some of the most picturesque vistas that New England, or any place for that matter, has to offer. Mountain peaks up to 134 miles away from the summit (Mt. Marcy in the Adirondack Mountains, to be specific) are visible when the skies are clear and the air is dry. On these sorts of days, the view from the summit includes five states (New Hampshire, Vermont, Maine, New York, Massachusetts), two countries (U.S. and Canada), one ocean (the Atlantic), and a plethora of notable cities and landmarks within these territories. Distant Vermont peaks such as Camel's Hump, Mount Mansfield, and Jay Peak can be viewed to the northwest, while Mount Blue, Sugarloaf Mountain, and Mount Coburn can be distinguished to the northeast. After the setting of the sun, when the valley lights slowly come into focus, the Maine cities of Portland and Auburn, New Hampshire locations of North Conway, Berlin, and Portsmouth, along with St. Johnsbury, Vermont all work together to dot the valleys with a white and orange feast for the eyes. On exceptionally clear nights, two broad but faint orange glows are visible on the horizons, signaling the bustling urbanized regions of Montreal to the north and Boston to the south.

Although the viewing of daytime and nighttime features are a rare and treasured event, it is the transitional periods that can result in the most spectacular skies the summit has to offer. As the sun sinks in the sky, its rays bend (or refract) through a thicker portion of the atmosphere, resulting in the appearance of different portions of the visible light spectrum. The addition of high clouds to the atmosphere, which are composed of tiny ice crystals, produce a much more dynamic show, with spectacles including a fiery red sky or illustrious purple streaks illuminating the waning hard day of work. When particularly memorable sunsets are imminent, it is the long-time tradition of summit staff to bundle up and head to the observation deck to grab a front row seat to one of Mount Washington's more breathtaking displays. After the day's closing glimpses of sunlight, the entire crew will head indoors for a hearty meal and a bit of relaxation before calling it a night. Although things change quickly and dynamically on Mount Washington, the staff can be sure of one thing—tomorrow will bring a whole new menu of challenges to face!

The Ice Storm of '98 Atop Mt. Washington

By Sarah Long – Portland, ME meteorologist
and former Mt. Washington Observatory Staff

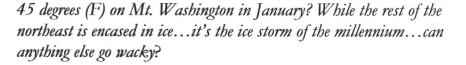

45 degrees (F) on Mt. Washington in January? While the rest of the northeast is encased in ice…it's the ice storm of the millennium…can anything else go wacky?

– Summit Log Book Entry, January 9

Freezing rain crushed trees, power lines toppled like dominoes, power grids crumbled like piles of melted slag. I mention this because the sides of the Auto Road are spectacular, trees bent in arcs and encased in glassy ice. The trail crews are going to have a lot of work next summer, but in the meantime, perfect photography vistas.

– Summit Log Book Entry, January 15

The Mt. Washington Observatory summit staff takes pleasure in working, living and playing in the "Worst Weather in the World." In January of 1998 several days of freezing rain would pile up enough glaze ice to be named one of the worst ice storms in New England history, and yet on the summit of Mt. Washington I was experiencing the warmest temps in the region, steady rain and watching the winter snow cover rapidly disappear off the summit cone. This scenario became the perfect teachable moment when it comes to how freezing rain works—cold air is trapped in the valley below while warm air moves in above, setting up a temperature inversion. The rain falling on the summit, where we were basking in record January warmth in the 40s, would fall into the cold air trapped below and quickly freeze to all exposed surfaces. As an Observer and Meteorologist I was keeping tabs on this situation perched atop the northeast at over 6,000 feet, but had little grasp on just how much of an impact this storm would make. The first clue in our solitary and soggy world on the Rockpile came when the chatter over the two-way radio started to pick up the morning of January 10th. Sno-Cat operator Chris Uggerholt, was shuttling a group of overnight EduTrip guests up to the Observatory but the snow tractor was quickly stopped in its tracks along the Mt. Washington Auto Road.

Hours and days of freezing rain had covered trees along the road with two inches of ice, causing their limbs to snap and many to come down across the road. The tangled mess of trees and branches was so thick the surface of the road could not be seen underneath and the road became impassible.

The overnight guests were returned to their cars without making

One of the more stunning types of clouds that are produced by mountains is a lenticular cloud. Many people have remarked over the years how they resemble space ships.

it more than a mile up the road, many of them likely returning to their own tangled mess without power. Chris and a crew of seven others worked together to cut fallen tree limbs, clear trees sagging under the weight of the ice, and use the snow tractors to remove logs and push debris out of the way. The team took several days to clear the road to where ice-covered trees gave way to trees showing little effect from the storm. The radio call came through: "Three-zero to two-zero. We made it up to half-way!" So our weekly shift change would happen after all. In order to take in the impact my shift partner, Lynn Host and I, decided to walk step by step down the winding road and take in the devastation caused by the ice. One of the most memorable shift changes in my long four years of traveling up and down to the summit of Mt. Washington each and every week.

Thousands flock to Nantasket beach, on the Massachusetts coast, to cool off on a hot August day. *Photo by Ann Kerwin*

CHAPTER 5: HEAT WAVES

New England typically isn't known for brutally hot weather, but that doesn't mean we don't have heat waves. In fact, most summers (particularly in July and August) we see an average of between one and three official heat waves. It is generally accepted in New England that in order to be an official heat wave, a city or town needs to reach 90° Fahrenheit or higher for at least three consecutive days. However, even if we fall a degree or two short, that doesn't mean it wasn't a hot spell!

INTERESTING HEAT WAVE FACT

There are only two states in the US that have never experienced an official heat wave. They are Alaska and Hawaii. Did the Hawaii part surprise you? Alaska makes sense, but why Hawaii? Even though the island is a warm tropical area, it is surrounded by cooler ocean waters, which very rarely allow temperatures to climb above 90°.

A popular saying, "It's so hot out there that you could fry an egg on the sidewalk!"

Photo © 2008 Stephanie Garza | www.genphotosaz.com

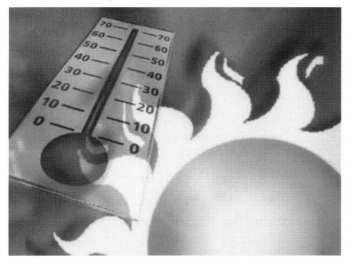

Heat waves in this part of the country are almost always accompanied by humid conditions, which can actually make it feel hotter. The *heat index* factors the temperature and humidity together to calculate what it "feels like" to humans. It's a little bit like the opposite of the *wind chill factor*. When the air is more humid, it isn't able to evaporate your sweat, which is why it drips down your face on hot and humid days. This of course makes you feel even hotter, because when sweat evaporates it actually takes some heat along with it. Why? Evaporating takes energy (heat), so whenever anything evaporates, it takes a little of the warmth from the area around it. Without this natural cooling function, the extra heat is more noticeable. When the heat index gets over 100 degrees, people really start to notice, and heat index *warnings* start getting issued.

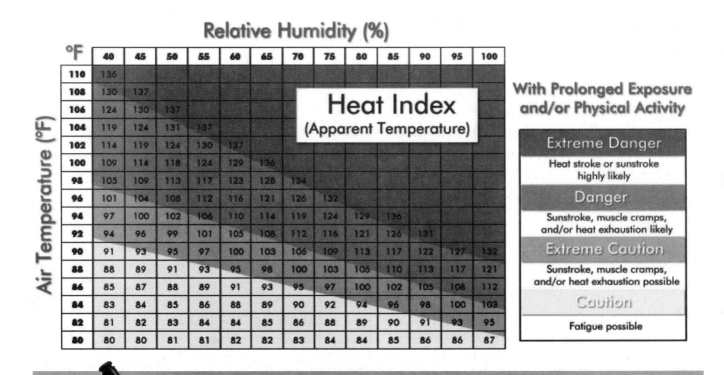

Relative Humidity (%)

Heat Index
(Apparent Temperature)

Air Temperature (°F)

°F	40	45	50	55	60	65	70	75	80	85	90	95	100
110	136												
108	130	137											
106	124	130	137										
104	119	124	131	137									
102	114	119	124	130	137								
100	109	114	118	124	129	136							
98	105	109	113	117	123	128	134						
96	101	104	108	112	116	121	126	132					
94	97	100	102	106	110	114	119	124	129	136			
92	94	96	99	101	105	108	112	116	121	126	131		
90	91	93	95	97	100	103	106	109	113	117	122	127	132
88	88	89	91	93	95	98	100	103	106	110	113	117	121
86	85	87	88	89	91	93	95	97	100	102	105	108	112
84	83	84	85	86	88	89	90	92	94	96	98	100	103
82	81	82	83	84	84	85	86	88	89	90	91	93	95
80	80	80	81	81	82	82	83	84	84	85	86	86	87

With Prolonged Exposure and/or Physical Activity

Extreme Danger
Heat stroke or sunstroke highly likely

Danger
Sunstroke, muscle cramps, and/or heat exhaustion likely

Extreme Caution
Sunstroke, muscle cramps, and/or heat exhaustion possible

Caution
Fatigue possible

Josh's Judgement

Walk into any room of more over ten people and ask how many people love hot and humid weather, and then ask how many people hate it. Quite often there will be about a 50/50 split.

Dangers of excessive heat

You may not even believe what I'm about to tell you. In fact, you may find that you have to go back and read it again, just to make sure you saw it correctly! Here it is: Believe it or not, in the last ten years, heat waves are the weather phenomenon that has caused the most deaths in the United States. That's right, hot weather led to more deaths than tornadoes! More than hurricanes, lightning strikes, floods or winter storms. More than any other single type of weather event. (See graph.) However, flooding still remains the most dangerous when you add together different types of flooding (e.g. flooding from hurricanes, flash floods, etc.)

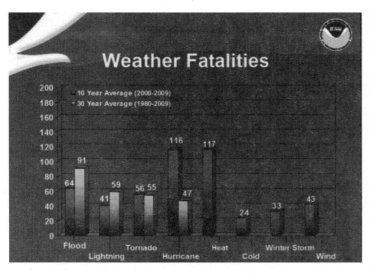

Compiled by NOAA

Those most at risk from heatstroke (hyperthermia) and other heat-related ailments are very young children and older adults, as well as those with serious illnesses. Quite often, problems develop when people try to do too much exercise in hot conditions. The body can run out of hydration to produce sweat, and has no way to cool itself down. When a person's temperature control system stops working, their body temperature rises too high.

During heat waves, young children, the elderly, and those with respiratory problems should stay in air-conditioned environments

When outside temperatures climb to higher levels, it's important for those at risk to limit strenuous activities and make sure they remain hydrated. Staying indoors in air-conditioned settings is also important, at least at regular intervals. Wearing light-weight, light-colored clothing helps as well. Lighter colors reflect sunlight and heat away from the body, helping you stay a little cooler.

Heat Index Heat Disorders

The following chart shows what disorders are possible for those most at risk, at particular heat index temperatures:

130° or Higher - Heatstroke/sunstroke highly likely with continued exposure.

105°-130° - Sunstroke, heat cramps or heat exhaustion likely and heatstroke possible with prolonged exposure and/or physical activity.

90°-105° – Sunstroke, heat cramps and heat exhaustion possible with prolonged exposure and/or physical activity.

80°-90° – Fatigue possible with prolonged exposure and/or physical activity.

Source: NOAA

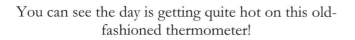

You can see the day is getting quite hot on this old-fashioned thermometer!

Know These Heat Disorder Symptoms!

HEAT	DISORDER SYMPTOMS	FIRST AID
HEAT CRAMPS	Painful spasms usually in muscles of legs and abdomen possible.	Firm pressure on cramping muscles, or gentle massage to relieve spasm
	Heavy sweating	Give sips of water. If nausea occurs, discontinue use
HEAT EXHAUSTION	Heavy sweating, weakness, skin cold, pale and clammy. Normal temperature possible.	Get victim out of sun. Lay down and loosen clothing. Apply cool, wet clothes. Fan or move victim to air conditioned room.
	Fainting and vomiting	Sips of water. If vomiting continues, seek immediate medical attention.
HEAT STROKE	High body temperature (106°F or higher)	Heat stroke is a severe medical emergency! Summon emergency medical assistance or get the victim to a hospital immediately. Delay can be fatal. Move the victim to a cooler environment. Reduce body temperature with cold bath or sponging. Use extreme caution. Remove clothing, use fans and air conditioners. If temperature rises again, repeat process. Do not give fluids.
	Hot dry skin. Rapid and strong pulse	
	Possible unconsciousness.	

Source: NOAA

Trying to beat the heat. Swimming in Lake Wentworth, in Wolfeboro, NH

Heat wave safety tips

- Slow down. Strenuous activities should be reduced, eliminated, or rescheduled to the coolest time of the day. Individuals at risk should stay in the coolest available place, not necessarily indoors.

- Dress for summer. Lightweight, light-colored clothing reflects heat and sunlight, and helps your body maintain normal temperatures.

- Drink plenty of water or other non-alcoholic fluids. Your body needs water to keep cool. Drink liquids even if you don't feel thirsty. (Consult your doctor if you have special medical circumstances.)

- Don't drink alcoholic beverages.

- Don't take salt tablets (unless specified by a physician).

- Spend more time in air-conditioned places. Air conditioning in homes and other buildings markedly reduces danger from the heat.

- Don't get too much sun. Sunburn makes the job of heat dissipation that much more difficult.

Source: NOAA

People keeping cool during a hot July day on Chatham's Lighthouse Beach and South Beach, Cape Cod. *Photo Christopher Seufert*

Heat waves cause other problems too

During such heat outbreaks, people use their air conditioners much more. They run them longer and turn thermostats down colder. This means electric companies have a hard time keeping up with demand and sometimes this leads to *brownouts,* a temporary loss of power because there isn't enough to go around.

Heat waves can actually cause physical damage too. Roads buckle, water pipes burst, and ice cream cones melt way too fast! (OK, that last one isn't really a major problem but it does upset my kids.)

Most often, New England heat waves form as a direct result of a "Bermuda High." You may have heard of it. Extremely large areas of high pressure, which generally bring fair weather, stall out with their center somewhere over the Atlantic Ocean near Bermuda. Since wind flows clockwise around high pressure, this puts us on the side that pumps hot and humid air right up to us from the Deep South. The weather is almost always hot down there in the summer, and the Gulf of Mexico is a good source of humidity.

Air Quality

In New England, poor air quality often accompanies hot weather. This is because high pressure areas that cause heat waves can also provide conditions that create lowered air quality. Sinking air that is found in these weather systems traps pollutants, preventing them from rising up and drifting away. A division of the EPA, AirNow, predicts the "Air Quality Index." You can see their forecasts and warnings online at: *www.airnow.gov*

Josh's Judgement

Don't always believe your vehicle's thermometer – especially on hot days!!! Quite often, your car's built-in thermometer reads temperatures just a bit too high. This is not due to equipment malfunction - rather it's because your car is usually over pavement. Ever tried to walk barefoot across a parking lot on a hot summer day? Hot top absorbs heat and re-radiates it, tricking thermometers. Sometimes they only read a couple degrees higher, but I have seen them as much as 14° above where they should be! By the way, when you're driving, the wind from the car's motion has no effect on the temperature reading.

All-time Hottest Temperatures for New England Cities		
107°	New Bedford, MA	August 1975
106°	Nashua, NH	July 1911
106°	Danbury, CT	July 1995
104°	Boston, MA	July 1911
104°	New Haven, CT	July 1949
104°	Providence, RI	August 1975
104°	Springfield, MA	July 1930
103°	Portland, ME	July 4, 1911
102°	Concord, NH	July 1966
102°	Worcester, MA	July 1911
102°	Hartford, CT	August 1975 & July 6, 2010
101°	Burlington, VT	August 1944
100°	Augusta, ME	August 1955
100°	Laconia, NH	August 1987
98°	Berlin, NH	July 1983
98°	Springfield, VT	August 1948
96°	Caribou, ME	June 1944
95°	Chatham, MA	July 1999

Notable Heat Wave Stories

July 1911: A deadly eleven-day heat wave struck the northeast, breaking records all over, many of which still stand today. Ice was the main way of keeping both people and food cool back then, so communities struggled to keep a supply. Across the entire region there were nearly 400 deaths directly attributable to the heat and many more indirectly. The intense heat buckled many rail lines, which led to train accidents and still more deaths.

Keene achieved 104° and Nashua reached 106° on July 4th, which still stands as the highest New Hampshire temperature ever recorded. On that same day, Vernon, Vermont hit 105° as did North Bridgton, Maine. Portland reached 103°, Worcester's all-time high was recorded at 102°, and Boston's record still stands at 104° from that day.

During the July heat wave of 1911 there were no air conditioners, so ice blocks were about the coolest thing around. Although…licking them? *Photo from the Library of Congress*

July 11, 1912: Boston ends its longest heat wave in history, nine days in a row of 90° or higher. This is an unusually long stretch for a coastal city like Boston, because at some point, a sea breeze usually kicks in to lower temperatures near the ocean. In this same heat wave, Vermont recorded the highest temperature ever in the state of 107° (in Vernon), which still stands today.

August 10-17, 1944: Another brutal stretch of blistering heat enveloped New England. For most cities, it was an eight-day heat wave, except Portland where the cooler ocean waters limited it to five days. Highlights include Burlington and Boston reaching 101°, Hartford got to 100°, and they even cruised up to 99° in Concord and Portland several times.

Jack Fultz (winner of the 1976 Boston Marathon) accepts a cup of water from a spectator. With temperatures at or above 100 degrees, it's hard to believe people were wearing long pants but after all, it *was* April.

Photo provided by the Boston Athletic Association, by Jeff Johnson

April 17-19, 1976: Here's something New Englanders don't usually expect: A heat wave in April! What an amazing run of temperatures, with three days of 90+ degree weather on Easter weekend. It started on that Saturday, the 17th, and by Easter Sunday everyone was baking! They hit 90° or higher in Boston, Concord, Springfield, Hartford, and most places in between. The next day, Monday, it was even hotter. Providence logged an unfathomable 98°. Others weren't far behind on that day: Hartford 96°, Burlington 90°, Springfield 93°, and Concord, NH, 95°. Further complicating things, the Boston Marathon was run on that day and the runners dropped like flies. A thermometer at the Hopkinton starting line read 96° right before the pistol was fired, and just kept getting hotter as the day went along. At the time it was dubbed the "run for the hoses," as spectators along the route sprayed runners with water in an attempt to cool them down. It didn't work for over 40 percent of the runners who had to leave the race early due to heat exhaustion.

August 1988: After an already sweltering July, the front half of August turned out to be record breaking. The first 15 days of the month either reached or nearly reached 90° almost every single day! In Hartford, only one of those days didn't hit the 90° mark. They were sweating in other cities too. Boston did it ten times (in the 15-day span), Manchester twelve, Springfield eleven, and even Burlington, VT, reached 90° or higher nine times. Even on the days that didn't get all the way to 90°, most of these cities were still well into the 80s.

Summer of 1999: Several monster-sized heat waves moved through the country in 1999, claiming 200-300 lives nationwide. We felt the worst of it here in July, with two distinct heat waves for most cities, three in Hartford! The region roasted through the July 4th holiday weekend, and on Monday the 5th New Haven hit 100° degrees, Hartford 99°, while Boston, Springfield and Providence all arrived at 98°. In fact, the Hartford-Brainard airport would see the century mark two days in a row, and then repeat that same feat again on the 17th and 18th. All throughout the northeast, rolling power blackouts were initiated by utilities, as people were running their air conditioners beyond the capacity of the power grid. The intense heat even damaged overhead electrical wires for commuter trains in Connecticut and many people arrived late to work.

Number of days in the summer of 1999 with 90° degrees or higher	
Hartford, CT	28
Springfield, MA	24
Burlington, VT	18
Providence, RI	17
Boston, MA	16
Concord, NH	14
Augusta, ME	10
Worcester, MA (Now that's impressive! Because of Worcester's higher elevation it's a bit of a rarity to reach 90°.)	7

A busy water park in Haverhill, Massachusetts on a hot day.

Summer of 2002: We were constantly seeking ways to cool down during the summer of 2002, as temperatures sizzled all over New England. Several cities saw as many as six official heat waves. Amazingly, the first one (for some) was during mid-April and the last was in mid-September. During one particular eight-day stretch in August (for some it was nine days), thermometers showed 90° Fahrenheit or higher every single day, including in Boston, Lawrence, Hartford, Manchester, Fryeburg, and Concord. That steamy summer, Boston logged 27 days reaching 90° or higher, Hartford 35 days, Manchester, NH saw 30, Providence had 25, and Burlington, VT achieved those numbers 16 times. Even the normally cooler Portland, ME climbed to 90° or above ten times that summer, very unusual for that city as hot southwest winds actually act as a sea breeze there!

2002 dates that reached 90+ degrees Fahrenheit in New England cities		
Hartford, CT	35 days	April 16, 17, 18 / June 11, 26, 27 / July 1, 2, 3, 4, 8, 9, 15, 18, 22, 23, 29, 30, 31 / Aug 1, 2, 3, 4, 5, 11, 12, 13, 14, 15, 16, 17, 18, 19 / Sept 9, 10
Manchester, NH	30 days	April 17/July 1, 2, 3, 4, 8, 9, 22, 23, 29, 30, 31 /Aug 1, 3, 4, 5, 11, 12, 13, 14, 15, 16, 17, 18, 19 / Sept 8, 9, 10
Fryeburg, ME	29 days	April 17 / June 21, 26 / July 1, 2, 3, 4, 8, 14, 22, 23, 30, 31 / Aug 1, 3, 4, 5, 11, 12, 13, 14, 15, 16, 17, 18, 19 / Sept 8, 9, 10
Boston, MA	27 days	April 17/June 26, 27/July 1, 2, 3, 4, 8, 9, 18, 22, 23, 29, 30, 31/Aug 1, 2, 3, 4, 11, 12, 13, 14, 15, 16, 17, 18, 19/Sept 9, 10
Providence, RI	26 days	April 17 /June 26, 27/ July 1, 2, 3, 4, 8, 9, 15, 18, 23, 29, 30, 31 /Aug 1, 3, 4, 5, 13, 14, 15, 16, 17, 18, 19
Lawrence, MA	26 days	April 17/ June 26, 27 / July 2, 3, 4, 23, 29, 30, 31 / Aug 1, 3, 4, 5, 11, 12, 13, 14, 15, 16, 17, 18, 19 / Sept 8, 9, 10
Springfield, MA	25 days	April 16, 17, 18 / June 11, 26, 27 / July 1, 2, 3, 4, 18, 23, 29, 30, 31 / Aug 1, 2, 11, 12, 13, 14, 16, 17, 18 / Sept 9
Concord, NH	25 days	April 17/ June 26 / July 2, 3, 4, 23, 29, 30, 31 / Aug 1, 3, 4, 5, 11, 12, 13, 14, 15, 16, 17, 18, 19 / Sept 8, 9, 10
Taunton, MA	24 days	April17 / June 26, 27 / July 1, 2, 3, 4, 8, 18, 23, 29, 30, 31 Aug 1, 3, 4, 5, 12, 13, 14, 16, 17, 18, 19 / Sept 9
Lebanon, NH	22 days	April 17 / June 26 / July 1, 2, 3, 4, 30, 31 / Aug 1, 4, 5, 11, 12, 13, 14, 15, 16,A11 17, 18 / Sept 8, 9, 10
Danbury, CT	18 days	April 17/ June 26 / July 2, 3, 4, 18, 23, 29, 30 / Aug 1, 2, 11, 12, 13, 14, 15, 17, 18
Burlington, VT	17 days	April 17/July 1, 2, 3, 4, 22, 31 / Aug 1, 11, 12, 13, 14, 15, 18 /Sept 8, 9, 10
Keene, NH	14 days	April 17 / June 26 / July 2, 3, 4, 23 / Aug 1, 11, 12, 14, 15, 16, 18 / Sept 9
Bangor, ME	13 days	July 3, 4, 23 / Aug 11, 12, 13, 14, 15, 17, 18 / Sept 8, 9, 10
Portland, ME	10 days	July 3, 4, 23, 30, 31 / Aug 3, 5, 14, 17 / Sept 9

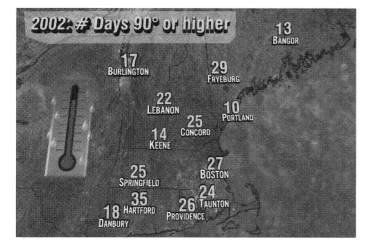

Number of days reaching 90 degrees or higher in 2010:

Hartford, CT: 34

Lawrence, MA: 28

Manchester, NH: 26

Boston, MA: 25

Concord, NH: 26

Springfield, MA: 23

Providence, RI: 18

Lebanon, NH: 18

Fryeburg, ME: 17

Danbury, CT: 17

Taunton, MA: 15

Burlington, VT: 11

Portland, ME: 10

Worcester, MA: 6

Summer of 2010 - The sizzling temperatures of the summer began early, with hot weather making itself known beginning early. On April 7th, much of the region reached the upper 80s and lower 90s, surprising many people. May and June brought several more hot days, and then the outdoor "oven" turned on in July as we baked day after day. During that month some New England areas recorded 90 or higher as many as 7 days in a row. On July 6th, Hartford CT tied its all-time highest temperature ever, of 102 degrees. On that same day, Providence also hit 102, Springfield reached 101, Boston, Taunton, and Danbury CT 100, Manchester, Concord, and Lawrence 99, and even the normally cooler Worcester airport touched 96 degrees.

Where there's a pool, you'll usually find lots of people on a hot day in New England.

Frightening Lightning! Bolts of electricity stream down over Lake Winnipesaukee in Meredith, NH

CHAPTER 6: THUNDERSTORMS

You hear the thunder and see the lightning. If you're outdoors, it's time to rush inside quickly before the pounding of rain that accompanies the dark clouds, which are moving in swiftly overhead. Some of us run inside and shudder in fear of the storms, and others get excited to watch the lightning illuminate the sky and see the wind gusts shake the trees. Whatever else is happening stops, as this storm now commands everyone's attention until it has pushed through. If it's nighttime, kids get up out of bed and run to their parents, and dogs bark at the window as if to scare away a predator. There's no doubt that these storms capture everyone's awareness while they are here.

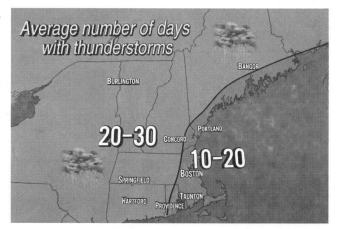

Although we don't have nearly as many days with thunderstorms as some other parts of the country, New England does average between ten and thirty a year. Eastern areas near the coast receive the least (ten to twenty); if you're farther inland there are usually a few more (twenty to thirty). That's nothing compared to places like Florida, where some areas of the state record over 100 days per year! There are approximately 40,000 thunderstorms in the world every day and about two thousand at any one time. Wow, that's very en-LIGHT-ning!

Coastal areas receive the least because of the stabilizing effect the ocean has on the air around it. Thunderstorms feed on unstable air that's warm and wants to rise, but the cooler ocean waters often change the nearby atmosphere at the lower levels. If you watch the radar on stormy days, you'll sometimes see fierce thunderstorms racing toward the coast, only to fizzle out just before they get there.

A thunderstorm (Cumulonimbus cloud) towers over Waterbury, Vermont

Thunderstorms form when there is unstable and moist air, and something gives it a "nudge" upwards. Most often, it's a warm or cold front that does the nudging. Other times it's the wind blowing over uneven terrain like the mountains and hills around the New England states. Sometimes hot and humid air has enough lift to start rising on its own without any help. Whatever gives it the initial start in the upward direction, unstable air does the rest by keeping on going up all by itself. As the rising parcel of air continues up, it condenses into clouds and eventually those tall cumulonimbus clouds that make up a thunderstorm.

You be the Judge!

You be the Judge!

QUESTION: What type of tree is struck most often by lightning?

A) Maple Trees

B) Oak Trees

C) Shoe Trees

ANSWER: B - Oak trees are often taller than surrounding trees, and have higher moisture content which conducts electricity better.

"Thunderboomers," as so many of us New Englanders call them, always contain lightning, thunder, and heavy rain. Those classified as "severe" produce hail, damaging winds, and occasionally a tornado. Whether a storm is "severe" actually has nothing to do with how much lightning is in the storm. About ten percent of all thunderstorms are considered severe. The National Weather Service defines a "Severe Thunderstorm" as one with at least one of the following: hail at least one inch (about the size of a quarter), winds in excess of 58 miles per hour, or a tornado. Sometimes two or even all three of these things happen at once.

Note: Until recently, a storm was considered severe if it produced hail of ¾ of an inch (about the size of a penny), but that threshold was changed to one inch by the National Weather Service on January 6, 2010.

The NWS defines a Severe Thunderstorm as one with hail at least one inch, has winds 58 mph or higher, or there is a tornado.

Josh's Judgement

It's not the rubber tires on a car that keep you safe. When lightning strikes a vehicle, the electricity travels through the metal on the outside of the car and then goes directly into the ground. This is sometimes called the "Skin Effect" as the lightning stays mostly in the "skin" of the car. This is because lightning takes the easiest path to get to the ground, and since the air inside your car is not a good conductor of electricity, it is much easier for the lightning to travel around it and through the metal. Obviously a convertible car would not be a good idea!

There are so many facets of these storms. Let's go through them all one at a time.

Thunder and Lightning

It wouldn't be called a THUNDERSTORM if it didn't have thunder. And thunder can't happen without lightning, for it is caused by lighting. Yup, thunder is the sound of lighting. How does this work? A bolt of lightning can sizzle up to around 50,000° (F). That's hotter than the surface of the sun! As the sky is instantly heated up that fast, the air where the bolt is, well, it *bolts*! That is to say that since it gets so hot so fast, it expands and evacuates the area extremely quickly. (Wouldn't you?) That rapid expansion of the air causes a shockwave that makes a loud boom, which is thunder. Sometimes as the air begins to contract and fill back in again, you can hear a lingering rumbling sound as it gradually returns to balance.

A tremendous bolt of lightning over Raymond, Maine.

Photo by Craig Clark

LIGHTNING MYTH: Lightning comes from the clouds down toward the ground!

LIGHTNING FACT: It's not quite that simple. When a bolt is about to strike, an invisible channel called a "stepped leader" actually comes down to the ground (at about 200,000 miles per hour), clearing the way for the lightning. After the channel is established, static electricity from the ground actually travels up toward the clouds (at about 200,000,000 miles per hour or roughly one third the speed of light). You heard right, the lightning actually travels from the ground up to the clouds. Usually this happens multiple times, which will cause the lightning to look like it's "flickering."

Safety

When a storm is near, the absolute safest place to be is inside a building. When you are outside, you are in danger from lightning. As soon as you can hear thunder, it is time go inside, as lightning can strike as far as 12 miles away from the storm itself. Once the storm has passed, the National Weather Service advises waiting thirty minutes before returning to the outdoors. If you are too far away from structures to go inside, the next best option is to get in your vehicle. Avoid standing under isolated tall trees or being in wide open fields. Lighting likes to hit the tallest thing in the area and that could be you! Also, stay off of boats and get out of the water if you're swimming, because again, water conducts electricity.

This logo is part of the National Weather Service campaign to raise awareness of the danger from lightning. The message is that as soon as you can hear thunder, you are in danger.

Because lightning can travel through objects even after striking its target, there are several precautions you should take during a thunderstorm:

- Never talk on a phone with a cord. (Cell and wireless phones are OK.) Electricity from a strike can travel through telephone and electrical wires. Also stay away from using a computer during a storm, as computers are connected to the electricity and often the cable lines as well.

- Never use anything connected to the plumbing during a storm. Don't wash your hands, take a shower or do the dishes. Lightning can travel through your water pipes.

- Stay away from windows and doorways, and off porches. You can still be hit by lightning there.

- Unplug electrical appliances, computers, and air conditioners. These can be permanently damaged by a power surge if lightning travels into your home's electrical system.

- If you feel your hair standing up (or see it happening to someone else), you are in immediate danger of being struck by lightning. If you can <u>instantly</u> take shelter, do it. Otherwise, crouch down and bend as far forward as you can. Grab your feet and keep them close together. You want to be as low to the ground as possible, while also taking up the smallest amount of space (as opposed to lying down and sprawling out).

You be the Judge!

QUESTION: About 90% of people who are struck by lightning:

A) Must wear a pacemaker afterwards

B) Will survive

C) Become electrically charged super heroes

ANSWER: B - Survive. Furthermore, almost all people who receive CPR shortly after being hit will survive, although they may suffer neurological damage.

Crash course in thunder and lightning

Cloud-to-Ground Lightning: Connects between the *Cumulonimbus* cloud and the ground. This is the most dangerous kind, since it strikes people and objects. As you read above, perhaps this really should have been called "Ground-to-Cloud Lightning" since the electricity actually travels up.

Inter-Cloud Lightning: Lightning that stays within the same cloud; it never reaches the ground. This is where the strongest static electricity is built up, so about 70-80% of all lightning is within the cloud.

Cloud-to-Cloud Lightning: Lightning that goes from one cloud to another but does not touch the ground.

Heat Lighting: You've heard of it, but do you know what it is? Is it lightning generated by the hot summer heat? No. Heat lightning is simply lightning that you can see, but you can't hear the thunder because it's too far away. This almost always happens at night because you can see the "flash" of the bolt from farther away in the dark sky, sometimes up to 100 miles away. Usually you can't actually see the bolt itself, just the sky lighting up. Truth be told, the "heat" part of the name probably only exists because most often this happens on warm summer nights.

Bolt from the Blue: A bolt of lightning that strikes an area that doesn't have a storm right overhead. It's named because it sort of comes "out the blue" when and where you wouldn't expect it, because the storm is far away. These "positively charged" lightning bolts can hit as much as ten to even sometimes fifteen miles away from the storm, even in places where it's sunny. Not only are these lightning strikes often a surprise, but they are the strongest types, as their charge can be up to ten times more powerful than average lightning. The electricity from a "bolt from the blue" can be as much as one billion volts!

Distance Thunder can be heard: Even the loudest thunder can only be heard about ten to twelve miles away. Since "Bolts from the Blue" can travel that far, as soon as you can hear thunder, you could potentially be struck. Head inside as soon as you can hear thunder.

Josh's Judgement

Since thunder is the sound of lightning, they both happen at the same time. However, light travels faster than sound, so you see the flash before you hear the boom. Counting between the two can reveal how far away the strike was. Since sound travels a mile in about five seconds, for each time you count to five, add another mile. Therefore counting to ten means you are two miles away.

The Odds of Being Struck by Lightning:

Odds of being struck in a given year	1 in 500,000
Odds of being struck in your lifetime	1 in 6,250

Keep in mind: your odds are much lower if you follow the safety advice in this book.

Source: National Weather Service

Interesting Thunder and Lightning Facts

- Every year in America, there are about 25 million cloud-to-ground lightning strikes.
- The electricity in one bolt of lightning could power a 100-watt light bulb for over 3 months.
- A typical flash of lightning contains about 20,000 amps and several hundred million volts. Compare that to a standard household current of 15 amps and 115 volts.
- The average lightning bolt is 2-4 miles long and is ½ to 2 inches wide, although the biggest can be up to a few inches wide.
- A typical thunderstorm is about 15 miles wide and lasts approximately 30 minutes
- When lightning strikes sand, it sometimes heats it up so fast that is turned into glass tubes called fulgurites.

You can learn more about this topic and lightning safety at:
www.lightningsafety.noaa.gov

ABOVE: A cumulus cloud grows quickly over New England, soon to be another thunderstorm.

LEFT: One of New England's Doppler radar dishes (The WSR-88D). This one is in Gray, Maine. Other dishes are in: Caribou, ME; Taunton, MA; Burlington, VT; Two dishes outside of New England also cover parts of the region in Albany and Upton, NY.

Photo by John Jensenius

What is it Like to be Struck by Lightning?

We asked that question of these New England residents who have been!

Joan Biron - Wilmot, NH

Hit by lightning September 7, 1998

It was 3 AM. An electrical storm approached from the south and started my golden retriever barking in the basement, which woke me up. I unplugged the stereo, the television, and went downstairs to check on my dog and put the light on. At the very moment that I touched the light switch, lightning struck and I was stuck to the switch! The electrical current pulled at my arm and went through the whole house. Lights were flashing and timers started beeping. Then the "bang" came and I was released from the light switch. My daughter, Sabrina, saw the lightning come up from the ground outside her bedroom window. She said it was very wide and went up to the sky. Now my husband, Rick, awoke with the bang and heard me crying. I grabbed my dog, Justice, and cried as I was so scared. The computer, telephones, and other electronics were hit in the power surge and damaged.

I had no burn marks on me at all. Later when I consulted a neurologist, he tested me and said that my nerve endings were fried, but would grow back in time. I was told that the nerves make the muscles and the muscles make the bone density. I lost 35 pounds of muscle and my bone density was compared to a person 30 years older than me. And now I am left with severe rheumatoid arthritis. My faith, love of my work, and the support of my family keeps me going.

Wes Miller - Warwick, RI

Hit by lightning July 17, 1968

My family and I were on vacation and we all decided to go our separate ways for the day. I decided, "I'd like to climb that mountain!" After hiking much of the day, I was positively thrilled when I reached the broad, level summit. I spent a long time there, overwhelmed by what I was seeing. Every direction afforded a stupendous view. There was light drizzle, but no thunder, no lightning, no threatening dark clouds. Still – and now I tell you something I have never told before—as I stood there, I felt my scalp tingle and knew the slight buzz of electricity. I'm sure I did not understand at the time what a serious warning that was, that I should have scooted out of there pronto. But the thought flashed through my mind, "nobody ever gets hit by lightning," so I stayed in place.

It could hardly have been moments later when the lightning bolt crashed, striking me. Ker-powee!

I always keep a daily log of our journeys. Let me now pick up on my journal entry of the event as written at the time:

Awareness of an indescribably loud noise. Awareness that I am screaming at the top of my lungs. I am sinking to the ground. Realization that I have been struck by lightning. Loss of consciousness for how long I have no idea. Awaken. Look at my arms and legs. They appear misshapen. I try to move, I cannot move. I am paralyzed.

"My God," I think, "I am going to die up here. Kathy and Scott will wait for me all night. In the morning the rangers will come up here and find me. I've got to get down this mountain. But my legs and arms are broken."

My compass and light meter are lying beside me. I try to reach them, but my right arm won't operate. After a moment, feeling comes back to my arm. I pick them up and stick them in my pocket. I look down at my legs. Now they look straight. Feeling is coming back. I sit up. I struggle to my feet. My legs look OK, but they are completely numb. I start moving and figure whatever is wrong with them, at least I can move now. I am driven by the thought, "I must get off this mountain." After I move the first fifty steps or so, feeling returns to my legs. I am not hurt!

But I must get off this mountain. I start running. I run as fast as I can. I run full out, then slow down a bit. Then a bolt of lightning strikes somewhere and I am jolted by fear. I am terror stricken by the thought that I am the target for another lightning strike. I can't get down the mountain fast enough. I go absolutely full tilt.

Lightning strikes over Littleton, NH

Ⓤlocal

When I return to the campsite, Kathy and Scott are there. They say, "Tell us about your day, dad." I respond, "You tell me about your day first, because when I tell you about mine – Well, you won't believe it!"

I got checked out at a local clinic. On the soles of my feet were burned-two burns, each about the size of a quarter. Small enough, but these are electrical burns and they go deep into the flesh. It took about six weeks for them to heal.

There were black marks on the insides of the soles of my shoes and holes in my socks. Both my tee shirt and jacket had burn holes. But here is a stunner. The left pocket of my pants was torn open. Apparently I had my hand in my pocket when the lightning struck and in reaction flung my arm out so violently that it tore out the pocket. This is a feat of strength that I could never even come close to doing as a conscious act.

Harry Sessa – Branford, Connecticut

Hit by lightning on June 23, 1973

I was camping in Nova Scotia and was certainly in the wrong place at the wrong time! I had built a lean-to, which I was sitting in when lightning struck me at about 9 pm. The bolt evidently came along the shore, cascaded up the side of the cliff, and hit the shelter. There was a large beam just above my head which had a spike in it. It shattered the beam and hit the spike, sending the charge right through my head and out my bottom. I was thrown about 20 feet. Were it not for the rubber mat I was sitting on, I would have been fried. Burns (exit wounds) were on my butt and between wrist and elbow and I was knocked unconscious for about 6 hours.

When I woke up, I wandered aimlessly around the field near the shore where I was hit. (The lean-to was completely destroyed.) There was a lot of stuff spread all over the place. Then I found my way down to the local farmer's house, but with my head and nose bleeding and my clothes literally torn and burned, they wouldn't let me in. They directed me to a gas station three miles down the road. I stumbled back up the hill to the car where I lay on the back seat and fell asleep. Around 8 am, Pete Merkl, my college pal who was camping with me, found me. Lucky for him he was not in the lean-to that night, but nearby out on his own. He had slept through the whole thing!

He saw I was in shock and the campsite was destroyed, so he drove me to a clinic about 15 miles away. As it was a Scottish holiday, we actually ran into a parade where several Mounties on horseback escorted us to the clinic.

When the doctors called my parents, my dad hung up the phone thinking it was a joke. I stayed under observation for almost three days and once I stabilized was discharged.

I was a kid of 23 and in great shape, with the exception of retina damage to my eyes and having to wear sunglasses for about 6 weeks. After the burns healed I was given a clean bill of health. I did have considerable amnesia and it literally took years to gain much of my long term memory back. The bad dreams and memories were at their worst for about two years.

Oddly enough, a few years later on the same date, my house was struck by lightning! For a while there it seemed like whenever I got out of the house it was "Lightning time." I got off much easier this second time as it hit the burglar alarm and blew it off the wall of the house. Three of the last four houses I have owned have been either hit directly or trees within several feet of the house have been hit. Absolute truth!

Help for survivors

Lightning Strike & Electric Shock Survivors International, Inc. (LS&ESSI, Inc.) is a non-profit support group by and for survivors, their families, and other interested parties. Their website is: *www.lightning-strike.org*

eXtreme Weather eXtra!

A Lightning Miracle in Maine

In June of 1980, something incredible happened to Edwin Robinson of Falmouth, Maine—he was struck by lightning! Why was it good thing? Read on.

Ed was blind and deaf, the result of a tractor trailer accident nine years earlier. One night, Ed was in his back yard looking for one of his chickens during a thunderstorm, and was hit by lightning when he walked under a tree. The bolt blew the hearing aids out of his ears and knocked him out for 20 minutes. A few hours later, his sight was partially back and he could hear perfectly!

He later told reporters, "When I woke up, I felt like I was burning up inside. I had to drink ice-cold water for three days just to cool off. The grass around the tree was burned out and so was the mechanism in my hearing aid. The doctors are still trying to figure out what happened."

Furthermore, about a month later his bald head began growing hair again.

eXtreme Weather eXtra!

Jet Aircraft and Lightning

By Jeff Sullivan, Lead Aircraft Maintenance Technician with a major airline at Logan International Airport, East Boston, MA

So there you are, flying along at almost 600 mph, at an altitude of 35,000 feet. You glance out the cabin window and notice Mother Nature is quite busy stirring up a vast display of dark cumulonimbus clouds. You marvel at the sight as you take in this incredible show unfolding just outside this pressurized metal vessel you are flying in. Water droplets are quickly starting to collect on the outside cabin windows and are immediately blown off due to the fast, forward speed of the jet liner. The sky has darkened somewhat as the sunlight becomes filtered, indicating that the clouds are winning out. As you look closer towards one of the darker cloud tops, flashes of light within illuminate it. The jet now starts to be buffeted as it hits some minor atmospheric air pockets which cause the aircraft to pitch up and down and roll side to side. More flashes occur and now you can clearly see them as lightning bolts jumping from cloud to cloud. Suddenly the "fasten seat belt" chime dings and the sign illuminates, followed by a cockpit announcement asking all to return to the seats and fasten their seat belts. You realize and say to yourself, "Great—I'm in a thunderstorm!" The buffeting and bumps get worse and you almost spill your drink. The flight attendant call chimes sound as other passengers, not so lucky, now need napkins.

What started off as a relatively smooth flight has now become a little bit more exciting. The pilots have already contacted air traffic control (ATC), and utilizing the aircraft's sophisticated forward-seeking Doppler radar have charted a safe course around this vertically stacked thunderstorm. The jet now banks and turns away from the storm, heading for smoother, less electric air.

Now here's the question I pose to you: Were you nervous and concerned for your safety, flying in a pressurized metal vessel, soaked with rain, full of fuel, flying near clouds shooting out lightning bolts, traveling around 600 mph at an altitude of 35,000 feet? I think I know your answer!

But let me ask that same question in a very different way, from a technical perspective: Should you be nervous and concerned for your safety?

My informed and professional answer to that question is: absolutely not! Of course, that answer is based on my knowledge of aircraft systems and design, along with my 25 years experience as a Lead Aircraft Maintenance Technician, for a major airline, where I am currently employed.

Estimates have shown that each and every commercial airliner averages one lightning hit per year or at least one or two hits in its entire lifetime. Now that's a lot of lightning strikes that you rarely hear about in the news! That's because the last crash that was attributed to a lightning strike was back in 1967, when a fuel tank exploded and caused a plane to go down. Aeronautical engineers and designers have equipped today's modern jet liners with advanced lightning protection systems, to keep them safe and keep them flying.

Generally, the first contact a plane has with lightning is at an extremity point, either at the nose cone or wingtip. As the plane continues to fly forward, through the areas of opposite charges, the lightning transits through the aircraft skin and exits through another extremity point, frequently the tail section. The outer skin on most jet airliners is primarily aluminum, which is an excellent conductor of electricity and is the secret to safely dispersing the lightning strike and allowing its high current to flow through the skin from the first entry point to that last exit point. It does so without interruption or diversion into the passenger cabin, thus keeping both you and your flight crew safe.

This is done by using very heavy gauge bonding wires and jumpers between fuselage skin joints to prevent arcing and burning. All fuel tank components and storage tanks are bonded and grounded to prevent sparks, under very strict FAA (Federal Aviation Administration) certifications and regulations. Aircraft wiring is equipped with shielding and surge suppressors to ensure all avionic instrument and radio control systems are protected. Radomes, the nose cones of the aircraft, which house the weather radar equipment, are equipped with special lightning protection strips. Finally, static dischargers and lightning arresters are fixed to the trailing edge surfaces of both wing tips, the rudder and elevators.

These devices help to disperse the high current flow off the outer skin layer and safely into the air.

Here's the rudder of an aircraft that has been hit by lightning. It safely landed in Boston and was repaired without incident. Notice the two static dischargers on the top and left, which did their job.

Photo by Jeff Sullivan

Even with all these safety devices and systems, lightning can and has caused damage to many aircraft. In my 25-year career I have seen and performed many lightning strike inspections on several different aircraft models and types. I have witnessed and documented many burn marks and pits left on metal skin structures, seen communication antennas damaged and small burn holes in honeycomb composite structures and panels. One time, years ago, we had a flight involving a Boeing B-727 that arrived with a wing navigation light assembly blown clean off the aircraft's wing tip. In that case the pilots were totally unaware that their aircraft was even struck by lightning, as the jet had no issues and landed safely in Boston. Each manufacturer, be it Boeing, McDonnell Douglas, Lockheed or Airbus, has very detailed and thorough lightning inspections that must be followed if evidence suggests that the aircraft encountered lightning. To ensure the safety of our passengers and crew members it is very common to take an aircraft out of service to perform these extensive checks. We put the aircraft in our hangar, using hi-lift devices to inspect every square inch including the top fuselage and tail sections. Even if we don't find any damage, the check itself can takes hours to complete, as lots of individual power control systems are also checked out. Only after that, and any damage found is repaired, can the aircraft be legally returned to service to continue what it does best—FLY !

I love my job, the company I work for and the awesome crew I work with. Every day brings on different challenges that we meet with both professionalism and pride. It is our goal, as Aircraft Maintenance Technicians, to ensure the airworthiness of your aircraft so you can enjoy a safe and comfortable flight. So happy flying and oh yeah—ding, ding... You are now free to move about the cabin!

As this picture shows, rain can come down very hard during a thunderstorm. Taken during a severe storm in southern New Hampshire in June 2010.

Photo by Donna Judge

Heavy rain from thunderstorms

Torrential downpours often accompany thunderstorms. In extreme incidences, as much as five to eight inches of rain has been recorded in New England in a period as short as an hour! This is most likely to occur when the air is very humid, meaning there's more moisture to harness. When this type of rain falls from the clouds, it's simply too much for the ground to absorb fast enough. Flash floods can occur within ten minutes of extreme downpours. This is particularly true in urban areas where there is more concrete and less earth to soak up the water. Storm drains can't keep up or get clogged with debris washed in from the storm, and roads can flood quickly. Small streams can suddenly overflow, and even basements can flood.

LEFT: Driving in heavy rain from thunderstorms can be quite dangerous if you're not careful. Visibility is severely impacted. And did you notice the leaves brought down in this picture from Exeter, NH? Hail from the storm also litters the roadway. *Photo by Ed Bouras.*

RIGHT: When the rain comes down fast and furious, storm drains often can't keep up, as shown here in New Haven, Connecticut.

Photo Christopher J. Zurcher of Environmental Headlines

You can track heavy rain and thunderstorms coming your way on Doppler radar, at: *www.radar.weather.gov*

Strong winds and microbursts

Another major danger from thunderstorms is the wind damage they can cause. Usually, as a storm approaches, you'll notice the winds pick up as it nears. Most thunderstorms produce wind, but severe storms have even stronger gusts that can cause many problems. Trees can be uprooted, houses damaged, power disrupted, and more.

As rain falls through portions of the thundercloud (cumulonimbus cloud), the cold raindrops cool the air. Some of them also evaporate. In order for water to evaporate it must absorb warmth, which cools the air around it. When this happens, a big area of chilly air forms inside the cloud. As you may know, cool air is heavier and denser than warm air. Since it's heavier than the surrounding air, this cooler air bubble within the cloud suddenly starts to sink like a lead balloon down toward the ground. This is known as a *downdraft* or *downburst*, and once this wind hits the ground it fans out in all directions. If the downdraft is wider than two and a half miles and does considerable damage, it is called a *macroburst*. If the width is smaller than two and a half miles, it is known as a *microburst*, which is often even more concentrated than a normal downburst or macroburst.

This is a simulated microburst over an airport. Notice how the wind falls to the ground and then spreads out in all directions. Anything in the path of those winds is in danger of "straight line winds" which means they will push debris in the same direction. Airports are especially cautious, as they can cause major problems for airplanes.

Illustration by NASA.

Microburst and macroburst winds of up to 100 miles per hour or higher are common, and they can cause big damage. Sometimes entire forests full of trees come down, power lines and even parts of buildings are blown over. When the damage is seen from above, microbursts can often be identified because trees are pushed down in an outward direction from the center, all facing in the same direction. Damage is sometimes so bad that people think they were hit by a tornado. Checking the pattern of downed trees can help to reveal which it was. Tornadoes create more of a swirling pattern in downed trees, while microbursts knock the trees down in the same direction with their straight line winds.

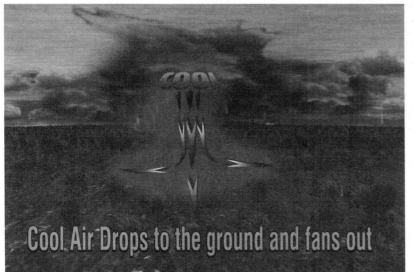

Cool Air Drops to the ground and fans out

As cooler air collects inside the storm cloud, it eventually begins to fall toward the ground as strong wind.

These trees have all been knocked down in the same direction, by the straight line winds of a microburst.

Photo courtesy NH Homeland Security and Emergency Management

These trees have all been knocked down a swirling direction by a tornado. Notice how the trees aren't all facing the same direction, as they are in the microburst picture.

Photo courtesy NH Homeland Security and Emergency Management

Hail

Many people young and old confuse hail with sleet. Both are ice that falls from the clouds, so it's understandable, but they are actually not the same. Sleet falls in winter weather systems. Hail can only come from thunderstorms, for it is caused by the intense updrafts that these storms create.

Even in summertime, if you go far enough up into the atmosphere, the temperature will drop below 32° Fahrenheit (the freezing point of water). Some summer days the height that you must travel up before you reach the freezing level is lower than others. When this happens, it increases the chances of hail when a thunderstorm moves through.

Another important ingredient for hail formation is strong updrafts. These currents of rising air are a key component for a thunderstorm to even exist, and when they are strong enough they can grow hail as well. As water droplets begin to fall out of the cloud, they are lifted back up by these updrafts, high into the sub-freezing environment. They collide with other raindrops, freeze, and fuse together. Instantly they grow in size and begin to fall again as ice, only to be lifted back up and melded with more and more water and ice, forming bigger

Pea-sized hail from a New England storm in 2003.

hail stones. Hail often develops layers because of this, and if you cut them open you can usually see these and tell how many trips up into the storm it took.

There's also newer research revealing that hail can form in other ways too. On occasion it remains suspended in up in the cloud, and does not go up and down as described above. These hailstones are kept up in the clouds by a steady updraft, and simply grow while continuing to accumulate more water and ice. This particular kind of hail doesn't have layers since it isn't traveling up and down in the storm.

Eventually hailstones are big and heavy enough to fall through the rising air and reach the ground. The stronger the updraft, the larger the hail needs to grow to in order to fall down to the ground.

The bigger the hail stone, the faster they fall. The strongest storms can produce stones bigger than grapefruits, although this is highly unlikely in New England. Extremely large hail usually falls in other parts of the country, especially near the Rocky Mountains because their higher elevation lifts them closer to the freezing level.

Because hail is created by raindrops and ice crashing into each other and combining, it usually isn't perfectly round. In fact, most of the time it is misshapen and "lumpy" or "bumpy."

Hail can cause damage to whatever it lands on, the extent of which depends on its size. Generally, it must be 1" or larger to cause big problems, which is why that is the size of hail which classifies a thunderstorm as "severe." Large hailstones can damage aircraft (both on the ground and in the air), cars, crops, livestock, and even roofs and skylights on houses. To make matters worse, can you imagine being outside when hailstones the size of golf balls are falling from the sky at nearly sixty miles per hour?

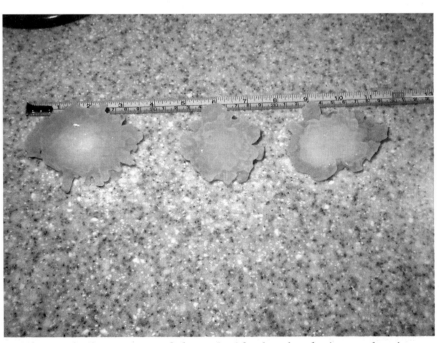

Often as hail goes up and down inside the clouds, it smashes into and combines with other ice and water, creating a "lumpy" look.
Photo by Ed Bouras

Interesting Facts About Hail

The largest hail can fall at up to 100 mph.

Hailstones sometimes have foreign matter trapped inside, like pebbles, twigs, leaves, tree nuts, and even insects.

When you cut hail in half, you will usually see rings (like an onion,) which can reveal the number of times it traveled back up into the storm, before falling to the ground.

Hailstorms usually last less than fifteen minutes (the average is six minutes), but their damage can last for years after.

Although Florida has the most thunderstorms in the U.S. they don't have the highest amount of hail because the freezing level is much higher in Florida, so hail often melts before it reaches the ground. As previously mentioned, the highest amounts are around the Rocky Mountains because their high altitude lifts them closer to the freezing level.

Hail stone sizes in inches

0.25"	pea
0.50"	marble
0.75"	penny/dime
0.88"	nickel
1.00"	quarter
1.25"	half dollar
1.50"	walnut
1.75"	golf ball
2.00"	egg
2.50"	tennis ball
2.75"	baseball
3.00"	tea cup
4.00"	grapefruit
4.50"	softball

Referring to hail by name, such as "penny" or "golf ball" size, helps others picture how large it was without having to get out their tape measure.

Notable Thunderstorms & Stories

So many thunderstorms occur in New England each year that it simply isn't possible to even mention a fraction of them. Here are a few stories...

eXtreme Weather eXtra!   **Frogs and Toads Falling from the Sky!**

As the townspeople will tell you, on September 7, 1953 an actual downpour of toads and frogs began raining from the clouds in Leicester, Massachusetts. According to the story, "the streets seemed to be alive with them and children gathered them into buckets." In addition to the streets, thousands of them were also found on rooftops and in gutters! Could this story be true?

There is much debate in the meteorological world as to whether this really happened, and some people think the story is a little "fishy." There's no doubt that reports like this one have surfaced hundreds of times over the years around the world, many of them verified.

The most logical scientific explanation is that powerful thunderstorm updrafts generate whirlwinds or even sort of a "mini-tornado," which can suck up and carry away debris (and frogs) in its path. Then, after being transported a while, anything picked up falls down with the rain.

Massachusetts Macroburst – May 21, 1996: A late afternoon severe thunderstorm moved through southeastern Massachusetts, leaving over four million dollars worth of damage. A macroburst is similar to a microburst, but covers a much larger area. That's exactly what occurred in Plymouth County on this particular afternoon, with winds clocked between 80 and 130 mph. They swept from Brockton to Marshfield, toppling thousands of trees, which of course fell on many homes and vehicles as well. Golf ball-sized hail was reported in Abington and nickel-sized in Whitman, some of which was still on the ground hours later. The line of intense storms then traveled across Cape Cod Bay to outer parts of the Cape, where more downed trees and smashed windows were reported in Provincetown and Truro.

The heaviest damage was where the winds first touched down, in Brockton, Whitman, and Abington. In Brockton alone, there were sixty people injured from flying debris or falling trees. There was also extensive damage in Rockland, Hanover, Norwell, Hanson, and Marshfield. There were many other surrounding towns affected, but to a lesser degree. Sadly, a young boy was drowned in New Bedford Harbor when his raft capsized in the strong winds.

Over 71,000 power outages occurred and some of those people didn't regain electricity for many days.

Thunderstorms as an Alarm Clock – July 15, 1996: In the early morning hours, a very fast line of thunderstorms roared through western Massachusetts and northern Connecticut. It is rare to have thunderstorms this strong so early in the morning, as they moved in between 6:40 and 8 AM. The storms produced downdraft wind gusts as high as 92 mph in Otis, Massachusetts, where one person was electrocuted by downed power lines. Many electric customers lost power that early July morning as trees brought down a lot of wires and even some telephone poles. Interestingly, many people said they heard a loud "roaring" sound like a freight train, something people often report hearing with a tornado. NWS surveys afterwards, however, found no evidence of a tornado and ruled it a microburst.

Widespread storms impact most of New England - June 22, 1997: On a very hot and humid day, a cold front crossed the region. It sparked many thunderstorms containing strong winds, lightning, and hail, causing major problems in all the New England states. The only state not to experience thunderstorm damage was New Hampshire. As a whole, at least 60,000 customers lost electricity that day, simply because of the storms. Several people were injured and two lost their lives as a direct result of the weather that day. Here's a rundown, state by state, of what happened on this stormy day.

Massachusetts: Severe storms moved through the southern portion of the Greater Boston area, as well as Plymouth and Bristol Counties. In the northernmost points of Plymouth County, wind gusts were reported at 104 mph. In the same area, just south of Peddocks Island, a 64-year-old man was knocked overboard and then drowned after attempting to take down a sail in the high winds. Lightning struck a landmark colonial house in Westwood, sparking a fire caused that considerable damage. In the Hyde Park section of Boston, a lightning strike ignited yet another house fire.

Rhode Island: The storms produced a microburst in part of East Providence (the Riverside section and Bullocks Neck) and West Barrington (the Bullocks Cove area). A boat was lifted off its cradle on land and thrown onto the top of a car, a crane was turned about 30 degrees in the Bullocks Cove area. A lightning bolt started a fire, destroying an upstairs apartment in West Barrington, and in Warwick, another strike ignited an historic clock tower on a school. Elsewhere, quarter size hail was reported in Coventry and strong winds overturned a boat in Narragansett Bay. Two people swam to shore but there were no injuries. Golf ball size hail was reported in Tiverton, while it was dime sized in Bristol and many other locations.

Connecticut: Thunderstorm wind gusts caused a 24-foot sailboat to capsize about two to three miles south of Darien in Long Island Sound. A 78-year-old man died after he was thrown from his boat. Wind gusts to 70 mph were recorded in Stamford, knocking down hundreds of trees.

Vermont: An individual was injured in Randolph when a tree limb was blown down and struck him in the head. In Tunbridge, an historic covered bridge was damaged when a tree was blown down on it. Wind gusts to 65 mph knocked down or uprooted hundreds of trees and damaged a farm silo.

Maine: Severe storms barreled through Kennebec, Lincoln, Waldo, and Hancock counties in the early afternoon hours. Particularly hard hit was the Oakland/North Sidney area, where numerous trees were felled along the shores of Messalonski Lake.

Martha's Vineyard Microbursts - August 8, 1999: A severe thunderstorm, which had just caused damage on Long Island, moved up to Martha's Vineyard and produced three midday microbursts from West Tisbury to Oak Bluffs.

The most intense of them struck at the corner of Ryan's Way and Edgartown-Vineyard Haven Road. At its widest point, it was approximately 1000 feet; many large trees were snapped at their bases. Side molding was peeled off a home, which also had its television antenna mast snapped in half. Damage to trees and structures extended for nearly three and a half miles, ending in the vicinity of Farm Pond before exiting the east shore of Oak Bluffs.

The second one struck a small area in West Tisbury, and downed trees of two to four feet in diameter along a path about a third of a mile long. Large branches were also downed, several small pane windows were blown out of buildings, and some shingles were removed from the roof.

A third microburst struck Dodgers Hole Road. It produced a very intense but isolated area of damage approximately 300 feet long by 300 feet wide. This area experienced downed and uprooted trees along with many snapped branches. One resident reported that a gas grill was thrown about eight feet across the deck of his home.

Severe storms cause a Bay State microburst and tornado, and put Exeter, NH through hail! – July 11, 2006: Temperatures were in the upper 70s to lower 80s across the region, a very humid air mass was in place, and a cold front was pushing through. These are the perfect ingredients for a thunderstorm to turn nasty, and that's exactly what happened in many New England communities on this day.

Thunderstorms broke out in Massachusetts, Connecticut, and New Hampshire, keeping emergency officials very busy this particular afternoon. A small tornado touched down in western Massachusetts in the town of Wendell, ripping roofs off houses and uprooting and debarking trees. A microburst was confirmed in Marblehead, Mass knocking down trees and lifting 30-foot sailboats out of the water and tossing them twenty feet. Large hail caused damage in other Massachusetts towns, including Framingham, Peabody, Salisbury, Newburyport, Auburn, Somerville, Billerica, and many others. In Connecticut, Berlin and Granby reported hail, and strong winds knocked down dozens of trees in many communities, including Glastonbury and Kent.

The largest hail was golf ball-sized and rained out of the sky in the southeastern New Hampshire town of Exeter. The hail was mixed in with torrential downpours and strong winds, causing a multitude of problems. One of the biggest problems was caused by the unusually large (for this area) hailstones that were damaging everything they landed on. One major problem was cars, as the ice balls dented their metal exteriors and shattered windshields. The storm passed right over the town's main road, full of car dealerships, making their sparkling new cars look like they had been parked on a golf driving range! In addition, area insurance agencies reported claims filed that day on thousands of other people's vehicles.

Exeter Hail Storm

By Ed Bouras, South Berwick, ME

I was driving into Exeter, NH for a job and hit the start of the hail. That forced me to pull over and wait it out under an oak tree. The hail got to over an inch in size and I feared my windshield would break. It was a wild ten minutes of torn branches and leaves and ice littering the streets.

When it was done I felt fortunate and moved on. Much to my surprise, just within the next few miles ahead, the damage was much worse – broken windows, destroyed gardens (and garden center), nearly every car damaged with dents and broken windshields, and flooding from clogged drains. It looked like a warzone with a stunned public wandering aimlessly and almost everyone calling someone on a cell phone. The sad part was that some house windows that had been around for over 250 years were done in by this storm. A car dealership had a total loss, the Walgreens had a collapsed roof, the lot of workers' cars at the Sylvania plant looked like a junk yard. It was surreal driving through immediately after all this. When I got to our job site, I was able to get several pictures of the largest hail I saw (see photo), and in one case I measured a flattened disc of 2 3/4 inches!

ABOVE AND BELOW: Ed measured hail over two inches wide. Luckily he had a tape measure handy.

ABOVE: Glass shattered in hundreds of cars; notice the rear window in the car on the right.

Photo by Ed Bouras

New Hampshire Microburst - The Day Before Bob

Meteorologist Mish Michaels

In the summer of 1991, I was working as a forecaster for WMUR in New Hampshire. On Sunday, August 18th, the threat on satellite imagery was clear—Hurricane Bob was sprinting up the East Coast. Just the year before, I had completed my degree in meteorology. Bob was to be the first serious storm in my short professional life. The tropical-born system was forecast to make landfall in New England the next day. Although the forecasting focus was on the advancing hurricane, afternoon thunderstorms proved more deadly.

That Sunday afternoon, a cold front slipped into the White Mountains, meeting up with tropical moisture streaming northward from Bob, at the time near the North Carolina coast. The atmosphere soon exploded vertically into a narrow line of strong thunderstorms that swept the southeast corner of New Hampshire with heavy rain, large hail, and devastating winds.

Around 4 PM, a group of people sought shelter from the soaking rain under an open air pavilion in Stratham Hill Park. According to survivors, at 4:35 PM there was a huge roar from the wind, followed by the loud snapping of 60-foot pine trees, followed by an earth-shattering crush as the pavilion toppled onto those under it.

Back in the WMUR Weather Center, I communicated warnings for severe thunderstorms issued by the National Weather Service, but to be honest, my focus was on Bob, a hurricane soon to make landfall on our shores—the first for the region since Gloria in 1985. Soon, however, the tragedy in progress began to unfold. The weather wire indicated a possible tornado in Stratham. Damage was severe and people were trapped under a building in a park. Newsroom staff scrambled to get the details. Just thirty seconds before I went on air to lead the evening newscast, the producer informed me, "Mish, three are dead, eleven injured." My heart sank. I felt like I was going to throw up or pass out. This was all too real—*it was real.* A horrible, devastating loss had happened. The thunderstorm was no longer a red blob on radar, it was a killer. I tried to compose myself and speak clearly as I fought back tears. Hurricane Bob was now less than 24 hours away.

At 3 AM, after sleeping an hour, if that, during the night, I was back at the TV station to face off with Bob. I was sent out to cover the wind and rain. Bob knocked thousands of trees down, left 100,000 without power, all but destroyed the apple and corn crops, sank streets underwater, and claimed two lives in weather-related traffic accidents.

By Tuesday, August 20th, Bob was gone, but the cleanup had just begun. I toured the seacoast with the Federal Emergency Management Agency, following along as they recorded the damage from the worst local hurricane in decades. But the true horror show was in Stratham. The vicious thunderstorms had left behind a war zone. Trees were twisted, cars crushed, debris was everywhere, and there lay the pavilion, smashed into pieces by the forces of nature. To date, I had lived through two tornadoes and marveled at many awesome storms—but I had just been a kid. This horrible tragedy made it clear those days were done. I had a serious job to do and a public to protect. Two decades later, my focus remains unchanged.

The Thunderstorm Dating Service

By Becky Guertin

I used to nanny for a family in Weston, MA on the weekends while I was in nursing school. On Saturday, June 13th, 1998 I left their house around 12:30 PM and started the trek back down route 128/95S towards Dedham. The rain was very heavy, and the road was quickly flooding. *(Author's note: that day there were multiple strong thunderstorms with torrential downpours. Nearby Norwood airport reported over 6" of rain on that day!)* I didn't get too far before I hit slow, bumper-to-bumper traffic. While I was sitting in my car just before exit 19, it died, completely lost power in the flooded-out road! Not knowing what to do, and without the hazards even working, I felt really stuck. I didn't have a cell phone and did not plan on getting out of the car as it was pouring.

Realizing I was having trouble, a Coke truck driver came to my rescue. He helped me push my car to the side and drove me to the Coke plant right off the highway in Needham. I phoned AAA and he drove me back to the Ground Round restaurant right off the exit, as it was an easier place to meet AAA. I waited inside the front door of the restaurant. The host that day was an attractive guy. He was also very kind and felt bad about my situation and that I was all wet. He brought me hot chocolate. Because of the rain, the restaurant was slow and we were able to talk very easily.

After about four hours, without AAA showing up, I called my parents. They first tried to start my car, which—of course—started right up, and then came to get me at the restaurant.

I had had such a nice time chatting with the host that when I got home I called him and told him that I enjoyed talking with him and that I knew he was new to the area and that if he ever wanted to hang out that I would love it, too. By the end of October we were an official "item" and then married three years later.

If it wasn't for the severe rain flooding my car, rendering it useless, I would never have met Steve.

A house in Epsom, NH is completely destroyed after a tornado in July 2008. Look closely at this aerial shot, and you'll see several rescue workers sifting through the debris, searching for survivors.
Photo courtesy NH Homeland Security and Emergency Management.

CHAPTER 7: TORNADOES

Simply saying their name can bring fear. Tornadoes are an amazing and deadly wonder of nature; in fact they are the most violent type of storm there is. They can cause incredible destruction in moments. A tornado's winds are among the most powerful on Earth, but they are also very concentrated, and can devastate a house while leaving the neighbor's residence completely untouched. Scientists have been studying these monsters for years, yet there are many aspects of them that are still a mystery.

You no doubt know that these powerful storms occur much more frequently in other parts of the country (like "Tornado Alley"), but they do happen here in New England too, possibly more often than you realize! Most states here average one or two tornadoes per year. Usually they are quite weak, but not always.

New England Confirmed Tornado Reports by State (1950-2010)		
STATE	**TORNADO REPORTS**	**AVERAGE PER YEAR**
MA	147	2.5
ME	109	1.8
NH	82	1.4
CT	81	1.4
VT	39	0.7
RI	10	0.2
Source: National Severe Storms Laboratory		

The technical definition of a tornado is: a violently rotating column of air extending from a thunderstorm down to the ground. It is not officially a tornado unless it is actually touching the ground. If it is hanging out of the cloud but doesn't reach the surface, it is called a *funnel cloud*. When there is condensation in them, you can see funnel clouds. Other times they are just wind, and therefore clear until they reach the earth and scoop up dirt and debris. Sometimes they have so much heavy rain around them that they are hard to see. These are called "rain wrapped" tornadoes.

The spinning winds in the strongest tornadoes can be as fast as 200 miles per hour or higher. That's greater than even the most powerful hurricanes. It's no wonder they cause such wonder and fear all at once! "Twisters" come in all strengths, shapes, and sizes. Some just knock down a few trees or branches, while others annihilate entire towns.

Tornadoes are ranked by how much damage they cause, which is an indication of how powerful they were. I'm sure you've heard of the famous "F-scale" or "Fujita Scale," named after Professor Theodore Fujita, who originated it. After many years of research it was replaced by the "Enhanced Fujita Scale" (often called the "EF Scale") in 2007. This scale was designed to better reflect the damage caused by tornadoes and more accurately rate them.

FUNNEL CLOUD NOT TOUCHING THE GROUND   TORNADO REACHING THE GOUND

The Enhanced Fujita Scale

There are six categories that go from zero to five, with five being the strongest. Less than 1% of all tornadoes are of EF5 strength, and that's a good thing. The newer EF scale is shown below, with the top (three-second gust) wind speeds, and a look at the average damage they cause. These rankings are assigned to tornadoes after they happen, as investigators inspect the wreckage. Nobody can look at a tornado and guess what its ranking is, until they see the damage it causes. This is because tornadoes can be deceiving as to how powerful they are.

EF0: 65–85 mph - Minor damage

Removes shingles from some roofs, minor damage to siding or gutters, tree branches break away or weak trees blow over.

Confirmed tornadoes with no reported damage are always rated EF0

EF1: 86–110 mph - Moderate damage

Most shingles or roofing removed from buildings, doors and windows blow away, some mobile homes knocked over.

EF2: 111–135 mph - Considerable damage

Most roofs ripped entirely off, even large trees knocked over or ripped out of the ground, cars lifted into the air, some homes shifted on their foundations.

EF3: 136–165 mph - Severe damage

Moderate to major damage to large buildings, houses partially or completely collapsed, heavy cars and some trucks lifted up and thrown, and bark stripped from trees.

EF4: 166–200 mph - Devastating damage

Most houses leveled, major damage to large buildings, vehicles violently thrown through the air.

EF5: >200 mph - Extreme damage

Houses swept away, skyscrapers severely damaged.

How Tornadoes Form

There are several ways tornadoes spawn, and some are very complicated and not even completely understood. The most common scenario is when the wind is blowing at different speeds or directions at the ground level and at higher altitudes in the sky. Let's say the wind near the ground is moving at 20 mph, but the wind one mile up is blowing at 100 mph. The

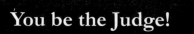

Faster winds aloft "push" air causing it to spin & roll

Faster Wind

Slower Wind

wind up top is pushing the air much faster. Imagine a barrel lying on its side and you start pushing just the top. That makes the barrel roll or spin, right? This is sort of what the wind does. Before long, the air starts to "spin" or "roll," kind of like that barrel, thanks to the strong winds aloft. This is sort of a "horizontal" tornado. Imagine how a tornado or a tube of air might look while lying on its side while spinning and you can picture how this appears. This is the first step to generating a tornado.

Next, a very powerful thunderstorm comes along, one with tremendous updrafts of rising air. As the storm, often called a *supercell*, moves over this rolling column of air, its updrafts lift that tube of air into the upright position. *Voila!* Now we have that same spinning air upright, and we have a tornado.

Water Spouts

A water spout is simply a tornado that is over water. If a tornado is over land and then moves over water, it becomes a water spout. They are usually weaker, but can still do much damage.

You be the Judge!

QUESTION: A tornado is most likely to occur:

A) In the afternoon

B) In the Morning

C) While You're playing Twister™

ANSWER: B - Most tornadoes happen in the afternoon or early evening.

TORNADO MYTH: If a tornado forms on the other side of a river from you, you are safe.

TORNADO FACT: Rivers and bodies of water seem to have no effect on tornadoes. In fact, when a tornado moves over water, it becomes a water spout.

A very famous photo of a water spout.
Photo by Joe Golden. Courtesy NOAA Photo Library

Josh's Judgement

An average of 1,000 tornadoes are reported in the United States every year. However, there are probably even more, since many hit unpopulated areas of the country and go unreported.

Dust Devil

A dust devil can look a lot like a twister, but is formed in a completely different way. They don't happen near thunderstorms; in fact, they usually occur on sunny days. Often they form as winds start to swirl around from differential heating from the sun, meaning that some areas heat up more than others. With the warmer areas next to spots that don't see as much heating, a swirl in the air begins to form and can cause a dust devil.

Safety

The biggest danger from tornadoes is actually from flying objects that are lifted and thrown by the wind. If a tornado is nearby, you should immediately seek shelter in the basement of your house or a building you are closest to. If possible, you should go to the corner of the cellar farthest from the twister. If a basement isn't available, get to a room with no windows; usually a bathroom works well if it's in the center of your house. The more walls there are between you and the twister the better. Additionally, many experts say you should lie down in the bathtub as its walls could help block flying debris.

A dust devil forms under blue skies.

Photo courtesy NOAA Photo Library

:

Most Deadly New England Tornadoes, 1820 - 2010		
Worcester, MA	June 9, 1953	94 killed, 1288 injured
Wallingford, CT	August 9, 1878	24 killed, 70 injured
Lawrence, MA	July 26, 1890	8 killed, 63 injured
Lake Sunapee, NH	September 9, 1821	6 killed, 30 injured
West Stockbridge, MA	August 28, 1973	4 killed, 36 injured
Windsor Locks, CT	October 3, 1979	3 killed, 500 injured
Hampton Beach, NH	July 4, 1898	3 killed, 120 injured
Great Barrington, MA	May 29, 1995	3 killed, 24 injured
Source: The Tornado Project		

Interesting Tornado Facts:

- The average forward speed a tornado travels is around 30 miles per hour, but they've been known to whiz along as fast as 70 mph.

- In New England, the highest chance for one to form is during the warm summer months. In Tornado Alley, the tornado peak is in the spring.

- A high percentage of hurricanes spawn tornadoes when they make landfall.

- Tornadoes have been reported in every state in America.

TORNADO MYTH: In order to be safer when one approaches, you should quickly run around and open all the windows in your house. This will equalize the pressure difference between the house and tornado, and minimize damage.

TORNADO FACT: This does not work and the extra time you take to open windows is time you could be finding a safe hiding spot and accounting for other people. Tornadoes will blow a window out in a millisecond anyway, so it makes no difference. The most important thing is to make sure you aren't near any windows, because flying glass does not feel good when it hits you.

TORNADO MYTH: A safe place to hide is under a highway overpass. Their strong concrete will protect you.

TORNADO FACT: In fact, this is a very dangerous place to be if a tornado is nearby. It is believed that a "wind tunnel effect" can be generated and many people have been "sucked" out and have died.

TORNADO MYTH: Living in a large city is the safest, because tornadoes can't occur there.

TORNADO FACT: There is nowhere in the world that is 100% safe from a tornado (although some places, like Tornado Alley, certainly see a much higher amount). Many cities have been the unwelcome location of a tornado in recent years, including Miami, FL; Atlanta, GA; Oklahoma City, OK; Fort Worth, TX; and Nashville, TN.

The Storm Prediction Center in Norman, Oklahoma employs some of the world's leading experts on severe storms and tornadoes. You can see their daily forecasts for possible trouble areas online at: *www.spc.noaa.gov*

Notable Tornadoes and Stories

Worcester, MA- June 9, 1953: Most likely the strongest tornado ever to strike New England (at least in recorded history). In the late afternoon hours, this killer twister descended upon several unsuspecting communities, bringing severe destruction and death. The vortex made a direct hit on the communities of Rutland, Barre, Holden, Shrewsbury, Sutton, Southborough, and Worcester, Massachusetts. 94 people died, 1,288 were injured, over 4,000 buildings were leveled and 10,000 people were left homeless. This monster was a mile wide, and traveled 46 miles in its 84-minute lifespan. Baseball sized hail was reported, and debris (books and clothing) was later found as far as 110 miles away on outer Cape Cod. Those in Worcester likened the scene to a war zone. Homes were literally blown apart, families simply shattered. One of the first things ever captured on MIT radar was this deadly tornado.

It also had an impact on the nation, as it sparked a re-organization of the Storm Prediction Center, and implementation of a vast radar and storm spotter network. This new system has had great success in lowering the number of injuries and fatalities in tornadoes ever since.

A view of the amazing damage along Pocasset Avenue in the Burncoat section of Worcester.

From the collections of the Worcester Historical Museum, Worcester, MA

One of the few pictures taken of the gigantic tornado that ripped through the Worcester area in 1953. *Photo by Stanley Smith*

Assumption Prep College took a direct hit.

From the collections of the Worcester Historical Museum, Worcester, MA

Worcester tornado memories

Meteorologist Bob Copeland, long time personality at WCVB TV, Boston, MA

It was Tuesday, June 9, 1953. I was working at the Foxboro Company in Foxboro, Massachusetts, at my co-op job connected with my engineering studies at Northeastern University. It was a cloudy, mild, early summer day, and I was circulating my mimeographed daily weather report to a limited audience in the Engineering Department. A strong cold front was moving eastward toward New England from the Great Lakes area. It had produced numerous thunderstorms on Monday and even a tornado at Flint, Michigan. My mentor, Don Kent, then known to most only as "Weatherbee, the BZ Weatherman" was predicting heavy thunderstorms for later in the day, especially if a warm sector was able to bust up into southern New England as a low center was scheduled to move up the St. Lawrence valley.

Taking my cues from Don, I put out a severe thunderstorm forecast for my fans at the Foxboro Company, and even mentioned the possibility of a tornado in the vicinity by late afternoon. Remember, I was just a weather nut at the time, not a professional meteorologist. But the tropical air did arrive on cue in the afternoon, the sun burst through the clouds and the temperatures and dewpoints shot up quickly. By closing time, we were running for our cars as a heavy thunderstorm pelted the area.

Early evening news flashes mentioned heavy thunderstorms with hail and strong winds in much of eastern Massachusetts and there were even reports of debris falling from the sky in the Boston area. The debris reportedly included some bank books and statements from Worcester county banks some 30 miles away. These were the first indications that something terrible, something unthinkable had happened–a massive killer tornado had struck the Worcester-Shrewsbury area. E. B. Rideout explained on WEEI that he felt it was probably a lowering of high altitude jet stream winds, but photographs emerged later of a huge funnel cloud and a damage swath up to a mile wide and 42 miles long all confirmed that this was indeed a tornado for the record books.

I drove that evening from my home in Taunton to Wrentham when I had heard on the radio that another tornado may have touched down there. I found and took photographs of several severely damaged homes, including one rotated 30 degrees off its foundation. I saw trees that had been snapped off 20 feet above the ground, others just skeletons with their foliage totally shredded and scattered over the debris-strewn landscape. It was my first close encounter with a real tornado. It may have been a separate event, or it may have been the dying remnants of the Worcester tornado, but its Wrentham terminus was less than seven miles from the Foxboro Company!

The Curtis Apartment buildings, destroyed in the 1953 Worcester tornado.

From the collections of the Worcester Historical Museum, Worcester, MA

A view from the air after the tornado wiped away much of the Winthrop Oaks neighborhood in Holden. Nine people in Holden died.

From the collections of the Worcester Historical Museum, Worcester, MA

Total chaos ensues after the twister moves through, everything destroyed.

From the collections of the Worcester Historical Museum, Worcester, MA

Damage to downtown Lawrence, Mass from a terrible tornado on July 26, 1890. The tornado reportedly traveled very fast, estimated at around 50 miles per hour. Eight people were killed and 63 injured in this rare twister.

Photo courtesy NOAA Photo Library

Less than three years later, as a graduate student at MIT and a Research Assistant in the Weather Radar Department, I was amazed to find a photograph of the first known "hook echo" to be associated with a tornado – the Worcester tornado of June 9, 1953!

West Stockbridge, MA – August 28, 1973: In the early afternoon a tornado ripped through the quiet community wrecking 37 homes and buildings, including a large truck stop and diner complex. Trees were ripped from the ground, powers lines brought down, and about 20 vehicles (including several tractor trailer trucks at the truck stop) were sprinkled about. Four people were left dead, 31 injured. Three of those killed were trapped in a small restaurant and a fourth was killed in a house two miles farther down the road.

A look at the tornado damage at a truck stop in West Stockbridge. Note the tractor trailer trucks heavily damaged, tipped over, and even peeled open like sardine cans.

Photos courtesy www.BerkshireArchive.com

Windsor Locks, CT - October 3, 1979: It lasted less than a minute, but caused three deaths, approximately 500 injuries, and up to 100 homes were destroyed. The twister crossed the northern part of Bradley International Airport and ripped the roof off the New England Air Museum's hangar, as well as destroying twenty vintage and a few commercial airplanes. The entire airport was temporarily closed as there were splinters of airplanes and debris littering the runways, and no electricity. That night, Connecticut's governor declared an 8PM-5AM curfew in an attempt to curb looting and vandalism. The state's transportation commissioner said, "It looks like it's been bombed!" Interestingly, there was never a tornado warning issued because it developed too close to the Doppler radar dish to be detected. (Doppler usually can't detect things within a very short distance, as the radar beams overshoot the target. This area is often referred to as the "cone of silence.")

An aerial view clearly shows the amazing damage sustained by the airplanes, most of which were part of the New England Air Museum.

Photo courtesy Virginia Welchvia
New England Air Museum

More of the destroyed aircraft from the New England Air Museum, which were tossed around like toys.

Photo courtesy New England Air Museum

LEFT, ABOVE: The hangar and everything in it was destroyed. In this photo, a private jet, helicopter, and several airplanes are thrown together into a pile.

LEFT, BELOW: More destroyed airplanes outside the hangar. The entire area looked like a wasteland.

Photos courtesy Windsor Locks Fire Department.

The Windsor Locks Tornado

By Terry Sutton

I remember it was a Wednesday afternoon when I was eight years old. My brother, a friend from across the street and I had left Norfeldt Elementary School in West Hartford early. It wasn't long after we got home that a terrible thunderstorm rolled

through. It was one of the most lightning- and thunder-packed storms I had ever seen. I remember the storm was unusual in that it lasted an hour or two but we were shocked when we looked at our backyard. The North Branch of the Park River was at least twenty feet from its banks. It was the highest I had ever the seen the river get, and that included storms that occurred after Hurricane Gloria and some terrible flooding in the middle of the 2000-2010 decade.

My father was at work at the time and called my mother to tell her that he was all right and not to worry. He told her that he had survived the tornado and would be home late. We had no idea a tornado had struck Windsor Locks. The building he worked at was near Bradley Airport in Windsor Locks and had part of its roof ripped off. Buildings nearby were not so fortunate to escape the wrath of a rare F4 storm. Up to this day, I still brag about how my father survived the Windsor Locks 1979 tornado. But I still remember that short and intense flooding that storm did to my parents' backyard.

New Haven County, CT - July 10, 1989: Several tornadoes formed in New England on this day. The most destructive one slammed into Hamden, Connecticut, causing over $100 million in damages and injuring 40-50 people. The twister traveled five miles, and dissipated just before New Haven. Witnesses described the funnel as about 300 feet wide. Over 400 structures were hit, industrial cranes and cars were thrown about, and an industrial park was leveled. Another tornado in nearby Waterbury, Watertown, and Oakville devastated around 150 homes and injured around forty people.

Hamden, CT after a powerful tornado does damage to trees.

Photo courtesy
Connecticut Urban Forest Council

There were several other much weaker twisters on this same day, including in the community of Cornwall, CT, where a tornado hit Mohawk Mountain Ski Area and removed every single ski lift. Several others touched down in Massachusetts, confirmed in Worcester, Norfolk, and Plymouth Counties. These tornadoes damaged several homes and structures, but luckily, injuries were much more limited.

Great Barrington, MA - May 29, 1995: A strong tornado struck Berkshire County, Massachusetts in the evening hours on Memorial Day. The tornado touched down in North Egremont and crossed into Great Barrington, where it caused the most devastation. Its powerful winds lifted a car several hundred feet into the air, killing its three occupants. Twenty-four people were also injured by flying glass and debris. In addition, the storm destroyed a gas station, approximately 75 homes, and the local fairgrounds. Newscaster Tom Jay was at the scene immediately afterwards, on the air at local radio station WSBS. He broadcast for over 12 hours that day and told his listeners, "The fairgrounds as we knew them are no more." Debris was picked up and carried as far as 45 miles to the northeast, where a racing ticket from the fairgrounds was found among other items.

The following pictures were taken by Steve LaPointe, Chief Meteorologist, WRGB TV Albany, NY, the day after the Great Barrington tornado. Steve got more than just the story for his viewers - he also brought back some great pictures that capture the event.

ABOVE, LEFT AND RIGHT: The main fairgrounds building was completely destroyed.

LEFT: Another building devastated at the fairgrounds.

RIGHT: Throngs of media showed up to cover the event.

ABOVE: The tornado scarred a large section of the side of this hill. The damage is still visible today.

Memories from the Great Barrington Tornado

Ed McCormick – Deputy Fire Chief - Great Barrington, MA

The tornado may have occurred in 1995, but to me, it still feels like it was yesterday.

I was on the way to my office on Memorial Day evening to prepare for the upcoming week, when I drove through a very heavy thunderstorm. My pager went off alerting me to a gas leak that I needed to respond to, so I diverted to the station and boarded a fire truck. As we approached the reported location, my driver said, "Oh my God!" and as I looked, I couldn't believe the complete destruction. Since we had been heading there for a gas leak, I assumed there had been a giant explosion. Buildings were destroyed and 125-foot trees were lying across the road.

Just then, one of my employees ran up to me and said, "My house is gone!" He was covered from head to toe in mud.

The top of a house was completely ripped off and moved.

Photos courtesy BerkshireArchive.com

Radio reports began coming in from other rescue crews around town. They said, "If you think it's bad where you are, you should see it here!" The roof had been blown off a nursing home, a school destroyed, the fairgrounds were flattened.

The next morning, I was able to see the damage from a helicopter and it was unlike anything I had ever seen, and that still holds true today. From the air I could see an unmistakable line of damage from the Hudson River to Monterey, MA. We actually got a little bit lucky in Great Barrington—if the tornado had been even just a bit farther north or south, many more people would have died.

A possible funnel cloud, spotted over Hampton, NH during a tornado warning in June 2007.

Photo by George Zeiter

2008 New Hampshire Tornado - July 24, 2008: It was the second most intense tornado in recorded history ever to hit New Hampshire, and left the longest path ever. The twister touched down in Deerfield, NH, and then traveled nearly 50 miles northeast. After Deerfield, it traveled through the towns of Epsom, Northwood, Pittsfield, Barnstead, Alton, New Durham, Wolfeboro, Ossipee, Effingham and Freedom. One person was killed, as her house collapsed on her; she died protecting her 3-month old grandson, who was not injured. Her husband was sucked out the window as he was running down the stairs to help. Another dozen people were injured. Roads were impassible because of downed trees everywhere. The tornado damaged 200 homes, completely destroying twelve.

John Jensenius, of the National Weather Service, surveys the destruction in Ossipee, NH.

Photo courtesy NH Homeland Security and Emergency Management.

Amazing bird's-eye view of the path taken by the July 24, 2008 tornado in New Hampshire. As the twister moved through wooded areas, it downed thousands of trees.

Photo courtesy NH Homeland Security and Emergency Management.

Note the "swirling" direction of the downed trees, from the tornado's circling winds.

Photo courtesy NH Homeland Security and Emergency Management.

A neighborhood in Epsom is decimated.

Photo courtesy NH Homeland Security and Emergency Management.

These cars are still parked in what used to be the garage.

Photo courtesy NH Homeland Security and Emergency Management

Hundreds of power crews were mobilized to restore the lines afterward.

Photo courtesy NH Homeland Security and Emergency Management

Print and broadcast media from all over converged in the damage area to convey the news.

Photo courtesy NH Homeland Security and Emergency Management

The 2008 New Hampshire Tornado

Meteorologist Kevin Skarupa, WMUR-TV, New Hampshire

Here in New Hampshire, we only average 1.4 tornadoes a year and looking back through history, we find that most of them are fairly weak. In other words, we don't live in an area of the country where we say on TV "Partly sunny and a chance of tornadoes this afternoon." On that fateful day the focus was more on the heavy rain threat than strong thunderstorms. Flood watches were in effect after some heavy rain over the past few days so (along with Emergency Management) we were on high alert which, as it turns out, was a blessing considering what unfolded.

My 15-year television career has taken me to places like Tennessee, Iowa and Florida where tornado outbreaks are a way of life and being on the air during them became "just another day" at times.

The storm that came north through southern New England didn't look all that threatening (except for the heavy rain) on radar. There were no gusty winds, no warnings, not even lightning being reported. But just after the storm crossed the border into New Hampshire funnel clouds were reported in Atkinson. Severe thunderstorm warnings were then issued which prompted me to break into programming, as we always do during those types of warnings. About 30 seconds into that interruption my boss came into the studio and told me to stay on the air—it was now a tornado warning. From past experiences, I know that is a situation where we stay live on the air until the storm is over and the warning expires.

It became so much more than that.

The actual tornado path started in Deerfield and ended in Freedom, carving a path through eleven different towns with EF1 and EF2 damage, at times with winds over 120 mph.

The pictures and video we were getting in from our crews and viewers were so compelling that we eventually just shut the studio lights off, knowing we weren't going to have to be on camera. The "break-in-programming" that started just after 11:30 AM went until the end of the 6 PM news without commercial breaks!

The anchors kept asking during coverage in mid-afternoon if it was a tornado, but there was no way to tell. As it turns out, the reason there was no video or pictures of the midday tornado was that the tornado was "rain wrapped;" that is, the tornado was inside the very heavy rain of the thunderstorm that produces it.

The National Weather Service went out to investigate the damage the next day. It didn't take them long to officially confirm it was in fact a tornado that caused the massive damage. It took the National Weather Service three days to confirm the entire 50-mile damage path was a tornado. It was labeled as an "almost continuous" tornado due to the complex terrain of the state which could have made it lift briefly at times. That 50-mile path is now considered the longest-track tornado in New England history (longer by a few miles than the F5 1953 Worcester, MA twister). You also have to go all the way back to 1821 to find a more significant tornado in New Hampshire; that one was an estimated F4 tornado!

Driving that path on my way to a talk in Wolfeboro a few weeks later was a sobering reality. When you are on the air you are seeing a computer screen; it's almost like a video game, not real. But driving it made me realize that it was a touch of tornado alley type damage in New Hampshire, not something you see often. And to know that the absolute power of weather produced scars of damage that will be there for decades is extremely humbling.

To this day I am still amazed only one person died in that midday storm that traveled 50 miles through 11 towns. It was the first tornado fatality in NH in 60 years, and for that you can't help but feel partially responsible. (You always play the "what if" game with yourself in situations like that.)

The really scary thought is, "What if that tornado had occurred about 15 miles farther west?" Instead of the eleven towns from Deerfield to Freedom, we would be talking about more populated areas like Nashua, Manchester, Concord and Laconia in its path. Instead of twelve homes destroyed and 200 damaged, it could have done even more damage and threatened thousands more people. Or what if it happened one month earlier with school still in session?

This tornado will continue to give scientists years of research as our New England tornadoes don't necessarily form, act or do the same things the huge Midwest tornadoes do.

The Terrible Tornado

By Laurie Plumley – Northwood, NH

One of my all time favorite things to do is sit out on my deck, look out over the water and watch the sun go down (or up). My dogs are usually asleep at my feet and the cat is most likely purring in the patio chair next to me. Neighbors out for a daily stroll wave greetings as they pass by. Relaxed, I recline in my deck chair and look towards the cove where Mr. & Mrs. Loon are proudly teaching their new baby to swim. Farther out, eagles fly circles in the air above as boats cruise the waters below. I close my eyes and breathe in the scents of fresh-cut grass and summer flowers of every shape and color. I listen to the whippoorwills, bullfrogs and other lake creatures sing their happy songs. (Insert heavy contented sigh here.) This is why I bought my house. It is also why I fight so hard to keep it.

On Thursday, July 24, 2008, at 11:47 AM, as I walked into my office, my cell phone rang. My neighbor called to say our neighborhood had been hit by a tornado. I asked if my house and animals were all right. "You have to come home!" was all she would say. It took over three hours to get to Northwood from Manchester. Stuck in traffic, we were continually passed by emergency vehicles (police cars, military personnel, fire trucks and ambulances) from all over the State of New Hampshire. I felt my heart quit beating when a horrifyingly huge 18-wheeler flew past me on its way to my neighborhood; on the side of its trailer, "Collapsed Building Unit" in big bold letters. Not a good sign. After showing a policeman blocking the road my ID and begging him to let me go, I ran down Route 4 towards my neighborhood. I could see all the utility poles lying in straight little lines like dominos in the road. I looked towards the area my house was to be and realized, out loud, "I'm not suppose to see the lake from here".

ABOVE: A photo Laurie took of her house after the tornado shows incredible damage.

BELOW: Laurie's house from the air (circled), taken from the state helicopter that surveyed the damage the next morning.

Photo courtesy NH Homeland Security and Emergency Management.

Panic changed to extreme fright! There were trees down everywhere; across the road, imbedded in vehicles and boats, and crushed into the homes of my neighbors. My animals, (three dogs and a cat) were in my house, and I went into overdrive trying to climb over the debris to get at them. I found my house. It was quiet, except for the rain. The devastation I was looking at took my breath away. Then I heard it. A bark! I hesitated before going into the house. They had been in their crates so I was not sure how badly they were hurt. In the back bedroom were my three dogs, each in their crates with tails going as fast as I have ever seen. I have never felt so relieved in my life. I found my cat in the corner of my closet, where I used to take her as a kitten. (I lived in Georgia where we had a lot of tornado watches.) Emergency personnel arrived to help me and my animals

out of my house and up the road to waiting vehicles to take us to safety. I not only lost my home and everything in it that day, I lost a big part of me too.

It's been well over two years since the tornado. I am back home, but not 100% complete. Insurance money has long since run out and there are major things that still need to be done to my home. I am tired of fighting with insurance companies, mortgage companies, contractors, suppliers and the like. I have been shocked by the kindness of complete strangers and hurt by those who I thought were my friends. I have done this all by myself. This experience has been more than emotionally draining, it has been physically challenging as well. I am not as young or as strong as I used to be. I have no choice but to keep moving on. What keeps me going on is sitting out on my deck with my animals, relaxing to the sights and sounds of the lake. This is what makes me happy. This is why I stay.

The View of the Tornado

by Linda Royer

On July 24, 2008, I was watching "The View" on WMUR-TV, Channel 9. At 11:30 AM., Kevin Skarupa broke in with a severe weather warning for flash flooding.

My thought at that time was "no problem, we've had flash flood warnings before." Within a few minutes, there was a huge bolt of lightning; the sky became eerily dark; and the patio furniture was blown off my deck. I had a gut feeling that this was no ordinary summer storm in New Hampshire and I needed to find a safe place to be until it passed. I quickly sought shelter along with my golden retriever, Buffett, in the innermost hallway on the first floor of my home and anxiously waited the storm out.

When it was over, I walked into the living area and found that a tree had come through the south side wall of the dining area and debris had blown all over the place. At that time, I was not aware that the roof ridge of my home had blown off, which I found out later was a good thing because if it hadn't, the entire second story of the house could have blown off.

I immediately used my cell phone to call my husband, Ron, to tell him that I thought he needed to come home because we had a microburst. He was in disbelief, thinking to himself, "No, there must be a mistake. It can't be real."

It wasn't until I opened my front door and saw the massive amounts of damage done to my neighborhood that I realized how horrible a storm everyone had experienced. The thought that a tornado had blown through our neighborhood never occurred to me.

I have always told my sons that I do not want to live where they live (in Tornado Alley) because of the severe weather people experience in those areas of our country. I also have told them that snowstorms are survivable. When it was determined that the storm that blew through New Hampshire was a tornado, I was extremely thankful to be a survivor; but guess who's eating her words now?

2009 Wethersfield, CT - June 26, 2009: A tornado formed along a cold front in the late afternoon, just before 6 PM. The tornado took down hundreds of trees, and caused over one million dollars worth of damage in a part of town with historic old homes. The tornado was actually somewhat narrow; witnesses estimated it at about 40 feet wide, and it traveled approximately two miles.

A stunning look at the supercell storm system that produced the Wethersfield tornado. This photo was taken of the storm from an elevated area in East Hampton, while it was over the Hebron/Marlborough area. Notice the wall cloud and rain shaft (containing hail as well) underneath.

Photo by TJ Demonte. All rights reserved.
Used with permission.

Many trees were toppled after the tornado in Wethersfield, CT.
Left photo by David Boissonault | Right photo by Raymond Hinchcliffe

The Wethersfield Tornado

Meteorologist Darren Sweeney, NBC Connecticut, WVIT-TV, Hartford, CT

Many meteorologists will tell you they've had an interest in weather since they can remember. For me, that's the case. I was always fascinated with weather and growing up here in New England (born and raised in West Hartford, CT), I was fascinated with the constant weather extremes.

June 26, 2009, was not your average Friday. I'm usually the weekend guy, but I had agreed to fill in for our Chief Meteorologist that evening. Earlier in the day I clearly remember driving down New Britain Avenue in West Hartford on my way to the station. I left my niece's graduation early because I had this feeling. I can't explain what the feeling was; I just felt that day was not going to be an ordinary broadcast day. As a side note, the summer began with an active pattern with an extended period of thunderstorm days, heavy rain and several bouts of severe weather. A cold front was moving through this day, so the initial threat for severe weather was there.

I arrived at the station early, around 1 PM, and saw just a couple of thunderstorms forming west of the Hudson Valley in New York State. Everything seemed normal about the storms as they approached. Without getting too technical I noticed the echo intensity (dbz's or decibels) increasing at an alarming rate. In other words, with each scan the radar was showing the storms were literally exploding as they entered the state. I clearly remember our receptionist coming into my office telling me that a viewer called in from Barkhamsted, CT to report "massive hail." When these reports come in you have to take them in stride. Here in CT, large hail isn't common. I've had reports of "massive hail" before when in fact it was only pea- or nickel-sized hail. That being said, I didn't like what I was seeing on radar and I told our crew we needed to go live to alert the viewers.

Just after 3:30 PM I went on the air to alert our viewers that strong thunderstorms were moving into the state and growing more intense as they worked south and east. Just after I got off the air I walked into our weather office and noticed the storms were not only getting intense but they were moving quickly east and were right on our doorstep. Within seconds the sky outside our studio became the darkest I've ever seen it. The streetlights came on and the fiercest lightning began to occur. At the same time our station took a huge hit of both lightning and wind. Not only did we lose power but we also lost the ability to get on the air to warn our viewers. We also saw outside in our parking lot something out of the ordinary for the state of CT: golf ball-sized hail was falling on top of our cars. I recalled the phone call I got minutes earlier regarding massive hail; it was now falling on our cars in the parking lot. I've never felt so many emotions at once. My first instinct was to get on the air. Our engineering staff was able to get us back on the air with a light and a camera and I was able to get some of my data back online.

Once back on the air, we were on the air until 6:30 without a break. We tracked the storms that moved over our station in West Hartford and then finally the same line that spawned the tornado in Wethersfield, CT. While on the air, reports of large trees down began to surface in a couple of towns, specifically Wethersfield. I clearly remember one of our reporters phoning in a report from a business on the Silas Deane Highway that had a kayak sucked out of their front window. Having worked through hurricanes in Florida and other severe weather here in the Northeast, I had never seen nor heard the type of reports that were coming so quickly.

After our non-stop coverage was over and the danger had passed, I compiled a list of the most vivid and descriptive viewer and reporter accounts of damage and I sent them up to the National Weather Service in Taunton, MA. I also gave them a call. They said they would be in the area the following day to survey the damage.

The following day the National Weather Service released their findings that an EF1 tornado touched down in the Historic Town of Wethersfield, CT, right around 4 PM. Winds were estimated to have been between 80-100 MPH. To those in Tornado Alley this might seem like small beans, but for us it was something that didn't happen all too often. The storm also hit a town that is known for its historic homes and trees, some more than 100 years old.

If you've ever wondered, "How does the National Weather Service figure out if it was a tornado or not?" take a look at this narrative from the National Weather Service Office out of Taunton, MA, following their investigation. It's quite interesting:

A narrow tornado moved through Wethersfield. The NWS storm survey team found damage beginning near the intersection of Nott Street and Park Avenue and continuing southeast into a cornfield along Elm Street, between Maple Street and Interstate 91. Along this track, numerous trees were downed. One of these trees fell onto a car on Park Avenue, trapping a person. Another fallen tree blocked the exit ramp of Exit 24 on Interstate 91. Many of these trees were large, healthy oak trees that were sliced in half, sheared off at their bases, or uprooted. One tree fell onto a house with such force it split the house in half. Two of the residents were inside the house at the time, but escaped without injury. One injury indirectly occurred as a result of this tornado, when a split branch high up in a tree fell the following day, striking a person. In the cornfield at the end of the tornado track, cornstalks were found flattened in a criss-cross pattern.

It wasn't the biggest tornado to hit Connecticut. As you've read, the 1979 tornado that hit the town of Windsor Locks was memorable. Ten years after that, in 1989, another violent tornado outbreak occurred. Several tornados touched down that day; two were rated an F4! The tornados touched down from the Northwest County of Litchfield, CT, south to New Haven County. The tornado touchdowns on this day were long-lived touchdowns, some lasting for miles. This is extremely rare for New England. In comparison, the Wethersfield Tornado was only on the ground for about a quick three minutes and it traveled about two miles.

It was a day in broadcasting I'll never forget (to say the least). I'm glad I was there working with a staff that had the commitment and experience to keep people safe. The one good thing that will come out of the '09 Wethersfield Tornado is that a whole new generation now sees just how powerful Mother Nature can be. It shows them that tornadoes can and do happen here.

We sometimes get complacent here in New England. Luckily, no fatalities were reported with this violent storm. I'm hoping books like Extreme Weather keep readers well informed, so they're even more prepared when (not if) the next 'weather extreme' effects New England.

Editor's Note: Darren won a Society of Professional Journalist award in 2010 for "spot news" for his coverage of the Wethersfield Tornado on television.

Weary from Weathering Wethersfield

By David Boissonault

A tree fell and split this house in half.

My wife and I were working on our garden at my parents' house, when the sky to the northwest turned a very ominous black. We left immediately to try and beat the storm home (we live 15 minutes away). We got to within two miles of our home when I noticed the sky looked unlike any color storm sky I had ever seen. That's when the elements let loose.

We were now one mile away from our home when the torrential rains started, but this rain was falling sideways, and the winds picked up very quickly. We continued to drive on even though we could barely see out of the car. We were following the taillights of the car in front of us. About half a mile from our home, we had to pull over as I could no longer see. The rain was windswept to the point that it was a whiteout. The only thing I could see was a wall of rain, leaves, and small branches blowing at us. That is when the hail started. It started at full force and that is when I knew this was no ordinary thunderstorm, this was much more. Hail varied from nickel-sized to some being slightly larger than a golf ball.

It was hitting the Jeep at such force I thought for sure the windshield would crack. I could now see trees from the yards around us falling and being uprooted. At this point I knew it had to be a tornado and there was no way I was sitting put in this. I started to drive forward at five mph, going around trees, downed power lines, and huge branches. It took about five minutes to go that last half-mile, and when we got home, hail was still falling but things had quieted down tremendously. We were without power for the next three days, and that night was the eeriest night as all you could hear for the next several hours were sirens and chainsaws. An evening not to be soon forgotten!

A photo taken by David of crews cleaning up trees and power lines blocking the road.

2010 "Tornado Watch Weekend" – June 5 & 6th, 2010: During this particular weekend, tornado watches were issued for a large portion of New England both Saturday and Sunday afternoons. Tornado watches do occasionally happen here, but it is extremely rare to have them two days in a row, which caught many New Englanders off-guard.

Three relatively weak tornadoes did end up touching down, one each in Vermont, New Hampshire, and Maine. A funnel cloud was also spotted over Windsor Locks, Connecticut but it is not thought to have reached the ground as a tornado.

In addition, a macroburst was confirmed in Massachusetts with winds between 60 and 80 mph. Hardest hit communities included Boston, Framingham, Natick, Watertown, Belmont, Brookline, Revere, Saugus, and Lynn. Boston's Logan Airport measured a wind gust of 68 MPH.

Here are the tornadoes that were produced, all from the same supercell storm, on Saturday afternoon:

Vermont: The storm first hit Orleans County, in the town of Craftsbury. A tornado touched down and partially ripped the roof off a home as well as uprooting many trees. It traveled about a mile before it dissipated, and was 200-300 feet wide.

New Hampshire: A twister was confirmed in Coos County in Gorham. The weak tornado brought down many trees, as well as a shed roof and roofing materials from a house. This tornado was estimated at 40 yards wide and traveled just a tenth of a mile.

Maine: The same storm continued on to Oxford County in Maine, and created another tornado in the community of South Paris. The National Weather Service survey team found numerous trees and structures with damage.

On top of all that, a microburst accompanied a severe storm in Harrisville, New Hampshire, on Sunday, with winds estimated between 100-110 mph. Hundreds of trees and about a dozen buildings were damaged. A funnel cloud was also spotted by witnesses, but did not reach the ground.

Cellphone pictures of a tornado over Gorham, NH in June 2010. It left EF0 damage, and luckily no one was injured.

Photos courtesy Ulocal.wmur.com

Ⓤlocal

Trees down on Beacon Hill in downtown Boston. A macroburst affected Boston and eight surrounding cities. *Photo by Lorianne DiSabato*

Trees that were knocked down in the Harrisville, NH microburst on June 6, 2010. Notice how they all fell down in the same direction, indicating "straight line winds."

Photos courtesy Ulocal.wmur.com

A telephone pole in Newton, Mass. snapped during the macroburst.

Photo by Lorianne DiSabato

Hardly Headed Home in Harrisvile

By Connie Lester

On Sunday afternoon my two Yorkies and I left Peterborough for Mom's house in Sullivan as we do every Sunday. In transit I heard a weather report stating both a tornado watch and a severe thunderstorm warning for Cheshire County, and called Mom to relay the word.

As I traveled through Harrisville along Child's Bog the rain started coming down hard, limiting visibility. My soft-top convertible Miata magnifies the sound of pounding rain so I slowed down to pull over, afraid other motorists wouldn't see me due to poor visibility. The trees along that road usually form a leafy canopy but were blowing wildly, and the ones to my left were at an angle I'm sure wasn't normal. I was definitely intersecting with some sort of weather event, and scrambled for the hazard lights (realizing I had no idea where they were!).

I looked up just in time to see a huge tree gracefully falling in front of my hood, taking the wires down next to me. I came to a stop, threw the car into reverse to "get out of Dodge," when another tree came crashing down over my trunk. I wasn't going anywhere. Cell service is notoriously poor through this stretch, but I had enough signal to make a call and did what anyone would do—I called Mom.

I screamed over and over that I was in a tornado (later to be deemed a microburst) as it was only minutes after my call relaying the forecast. I then called 911 and was unable to respond intelligently. Thank goodness for GPS in cell phones, because I knew my visual description wasn't what they needed, and then I lost service. Branches, sticks and debris were pummeling the car and there were still five or six more leaning oak trees next to me that could still come down. I had nowhere to escape. Both Mom and the people at 911 asked if I was OK, but answering seemed premature as one more falling tree could change everything. The world went white for a minute like we were in a sparkling fog, but after a very long two or three minutes the winds calmed. My dogs, Bernadette and Ruby, seemed invisible during this time, and I wonder if they knew something was very wrong.

The first motorist to arrive on the scene was Bruce Adams, an insurance man I knew from Keene. After he announced his name and learned I was OK, we both breathed huge sighs of relief. From his perspective through the branches, he thought for sure there would be injuries. Soon Kevin Smith from the Harrisville Fire Department arrived and took me and the dogs into his truck. Another volunteer, Roberta Gline, took me back to the Fire Department where I could stay until PSNH could cut my car out.

Slowly calls came in about other places in town with damage and downed trees, and it became apparent I would be there a while. After several hours a group of volunteers helped deliver me and the two dogs on foot to my family who were viewing the damage on the Nelson side of the impassable swath of destruction, just a half-mile from where my car was stranded. If I could just get to them they wouldn't need to travel 25 miles via Keene to get me. With the volunteers' help, we all navigated through the half-mile of downed trees and wires with two wet, scared dogs and me handicapped by flip-flops, but we made it.

The skyline has changed drastically, people's yards were destroyed, and homes and parked cars damaged, but this story ends without injury to anyone in the storm's path, and without so much as a scratch to my car. There were many lucky people that day, and I guess Mother Nature was only showing us what she can do.

Here's Connie's Miata, stranded after the microburst in Harrisville, after trees blocked her from both sides.

Featured Contributor

The Weather Boy

A true story, told by Fritz Wetherbee, New Hampshire's premiere story teller.

Back in the mid nineteen-sixties a tornado ripped through the town of Troy, New Hampshire. Barns were blown down, trees toppled; the slate shingles were blown off the Troy Town hall.

A huge chimney and fireplace were ripped off the Sanderson family home in the village.

Jack Sanderson was just a little kid then. He had gotten home from daycare after the tornado struck. He was playing in the back yard amidst the destruction, sitting on the pile of bricks that used to be the family's hearth when his mother appeared.

Devastation was everywhere.

Mrs. Sanderson had not heard about the tornado. This was all new to her. She was in shock.

"What happened?" she asked little Jack.

Jack's eyes got big.

"Kierston did it," he said.

All that is left of a house in New Hampshire after a tornado reduces it to rubble.

Photo courtesy
NH Homeland Security and
Emergency Management

Hurricane Bob moves over the northeast in August 1991. *Photo courtesy NOAA*

CHAPTER 8: HURRICANES

As this book shows, there are many types of extreme weather, but hurricanes are certainly one of the most destructive. I don't say this just because they are such monster storms, but also because there are so many ways they can cause devastation. Strong winds, heavy rain, and *storm surge* are just some of their fury. Hurricanes also often give birth to other storms within, like tornadoes and thunderstorms.

Just like anything in the weather world, hurricanes come in all sizes, shapes, and strengths. There are various types and categories to keep them sorted out, and these are the only kind of storms that we actually give names to.

You be the Judge!

QUESTION: What is the difference between a hurricane and a typhoon?

A) Nothing, they're the same thing, just different names.

B) A hurricane has much stronger winds.

C) Typhoons are only over water.

ANSWER: B - There is no difference, a typhoon is simply what they call a hurricane in the western Pacific Ocean.

The majority of these storms occur during late summer and early fall. The months of August and September have the highest frequency. Here in the New England area, we don't experience them very often, but that's not to say they never reach us. As you'll see later in this chapter, there are several major hurricanes that have paid us a visit and etched themselves into our history. Almost every single hurricane or strong tropical storm that has directly struck New England has done so in August or September.

Hurricane season begins on June 1st and lasts until November 30th. Wow, that's six months of the year! Although it's rare, they do also form before and after the official season as well. They usually begin during summer and fall because that's when the ocean waters are at their warmest, and warm water is needed for a hurricane to form. In fact, studies show that the ocean water must be at least 80° Fahrenheit for one to get started, and that warmth must also be present to at least 150 feet deep. Of course, as with everything weather-related, there are rare exceptions. These warm ocean waters and the moist air above them are a tropical system's fuel. This is why much of the time they are formed down in or near the tropics, because that's where the water is the warmest. This also explains why Florida, areas along the Gulf coast, and in the Caribbean are so often struck.

When hurricanes make landfall, they begin to weaken because they no longer have the warmer ocean water to feed on. However, their strength takes a while to dwindle, allowing much time for spreading destruction to anything in their path. These storms also weaken as they travel into cooler water, which is why when they steam toward New England they usually lose some of their intensity before getting here. Still, with their often fast speed of travel, they can be extremely dangerous.

Interesting Hurricane Stats

- There has never been a hurricane season without a hurricane.

- The smallest number ever for a season in the Atlantic Ocean was two storms.

- The most hurricanes ever at the same time, in the Atlantic was four.

- The fastest a hurricane has ever intensified was Wilma in 2005. In just 16 hours the storm strengthened from a tropical storm to a category 5!

- The longest a hurricane has ever lasted in the Atlantic Ocean was Ginger. It lasted 28 days, from September 6th to October 5, 1971.

Stages of Development

Most "seedlings" for hurricanes start as an area of unorganized thunderstorms. Sometimes thunderstorms begin over western Africa, and other times over the ocean. Although storms need to be well to our south to form, because they need 80° or higher water temperatures, they also can't be too close to the equator. In fact, the beginning of a tropical system must be at least 300 miles away from the equator or it won't be able to develop the circulation that makes it so powerful. North of the equator, storms circulate counter-clockwise and to the south, they travel clockwise. In between (over the equator) is sort of a no-man's-land where circulation can't really get going in either direction.

Once these requirements are met (along with some other atmospheric necessities as well, like a rapidly cooling air mass as you travel upwards and lighter winds aloft), a small percentage of thunderstorm clusters become something much more ferocious. As the winds increase, they start to climb the ladder of power.

Tropical Disturbance: A cluster of thunderstorms or area of storminess in the tropics. Also known as an *Easterly Wave* if it's moving from east to west. These disturbances are often the seeds for tropical storms and hurricanes, although most of them never reach that status.

Tropical Depression: A weak tropical cyclone (often starts as a Tropical Disturbance), with winds up to 38 mph.

Tropical Storm: Once the winds in a tropical disturbance reach 39 mph or higher, it becomes a Tropical Storm and receives a name. Tropical Storms have winds between 39 and 73 mph. The biggest problem they usually bring to an area is heavy rainfall and some minor wind damage. The rain in a tropical storm is often concentrated toward the center of the system.

Hurricane: When the winds reach or surpass 74 mph, the storm is now a hurricane. Once a hurricane, it is classified according to its wind speed on the Saffir-Simpson scale. When a storm reaches category 3 or higher, it is considered a major hurricane.

The Saffir-Simpson Scale:

There are five categories of hurricanes, based upon their wind speeds:

Category 1: Winds from 74-95 miles per hour
Small damage to buildings, branches will snap off trees and some small trees and telephone poles could be knocked down, causing power to go out in some spots.

Category 2: Winds from 96-110 miles per hour

House siding and parts of the windows and shingles on the roof may blow off. Older mobile homes can suffer quite a bit of damage. Some poorly built signs will be blown down. Many trees and telephone poles will be knocked down causing widespread power outages.

Category 3: Winds from 111-130 miles per hour

Many homes will be damaged. Some windows will be blown out of high rise buildings. Many poorly built signs will be blown down. Lots of trees and telephone poles will be knocked down and almost all houses in the area will lose electricity for days or weeks.

Category 4: Winds from 131-155 miles per hour

The walls and roofs of a lot of homes are destroyed, with complete destruction to older mobile homes. Most signs are blown down. Many windows will be blown out of high rise buildings. Hundreds or thousands of fallen trees and telephone poles will block roads and leave most areas with no electricity for weeks.

Category 5: Winds are above 155 miles per hour

Many houses and businesses are completely destroyed, blown over, or even blown away. Complete destruction to all mobile homes. All signs are blown down. Nearly all windows are blown out of high rise buildings. Most of the trees and telephone poles will be knocked down and will block areas off and cause electricity to be lost for weeks or months.

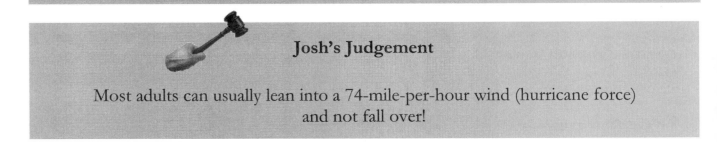

HURRICANE MYTH: The bigger the tropical cyclone, the stronger it is.

HURRICANE FACT: Size truly doesn't matter when it comes to hurricanes! There are often small systems that pack quite a punch. Hurricane Andrew (1992) was a good example, as it was a smaller storm but very deadly.

Josh's Judgement

Most adults can usually lean into a 74-mile-per-hour wind (hurricane force)
and not fall over!

Naming Hurricanes and Tropical Storms

A question I'm often asked is: Why are these storms named? That's certainly a valid question, but there are several good reasons. First off, it is for the ease of conveying information to the public in a manner that they'll instantly know what storm you are talking about. The same can be said for communication between forecasters who are monitoring and predicting weather. Using a name is much easier than saying, "Hey, that hurricane out in the Atlantic Ocean that we've been watching is strengthening and getting closer."

Also, quite often there can be more than one tropical storm or hurricane occurring simultaneously. Imagine the confusion in a scenario involving forecasters attempting to inform the public about three hurricanes that are all in the Atlantic! They would have to very carefully describe each storm's location and people would get likely get them mixed up.

Additionally, naming storms helps with identifying past tropical cyclones so people can instantly call them up in their memories. If I asked you, "Remember that hurricane that caused all that devastation in August of 2005?" You may or may not be able to place it. Yet if I call it by the name "Hurricane Katrina," you instantly know which storm we're talking about.

Even back before they named hurricanes, the biggest were nicknamed afterwards so that we would remember them. The Hurricane of 1938 is usually referred to as "The Great New England Hurricane" or "The Long Island Express," and the 1944 system is called, "The Great Atlantic Hurricane." During World War II, military forecasters began unofficially naming tropical systems in the Pacific. They usually named them after their girlfriends or wives (I hope they didn't find out!). Then from 1950-52, Atlantic Ocean hurricanes were identified by the phonetic alphabet (Alpha, Baker, Charlie, and so on). In 1953 the US weather service began naming storms, using just women's names. Finally in 1979, as is still done today, they began using both men's and women's names in alternating fashion. The practice was started by the National Weather Service and the World Meteorological Organization (WMO).

There are six lists of names that rotate over and over. This means that if your name isn't on the list, it may never be used. The exception is if a storm's name is retired. When hurricanes are exceptionally destructive, leading to many deaths, names are retired out of respect to the victims. When a name is retired, the WMO replaces it with another of the same gender and first letter.

Here's a list of Hurricane names that have been retired since the year 2000. For a complete list of every name ever retired, visit: *www.nhc.noaa.gov/retirednames.shtml*

2000	Keith	2005	Dennis, Katrina, Rita, Stan, Wilma
2001	Allison, Iris, Michelle	2006	*None*
2002	Isidore, Lili	2007	Dean, Felix, Noel
2003	Fabian, Isabel, Juan	2008	Gustav, Ike, Paloma
2004	Charley, Frances, Ivan, Jeanne	2009	*None*

Only 21 of the 26 letters of the alphabet are used, because each letter used needs to have a vast number of names to choose from, enough to replace retired names many times over.

Contrary to popular belief, meteorologists do not consult baby name books when thinking up hurricane names.

Hurricane Names for 2011-2015

2011	2012	2013	2014	2015
Arlene	Alberto	Andrea	Arthur	Ana
Bret	Beryl	Barry	Bertha	Bill
Cindy	Chris	Chantal	Cristobal	Claudette
Don	Debby	Dorian	Dolly	Danny
Emily	Ernesto	Erin	Edouard	Erika
Franklin	Florence	Fernand	Fay	Fred
Gert	Gordon	Gabrielle	Gonzalo	Grace
Harvey	Helene	Humberto	Hannah	Henri
Irene	Isaac	Ingrid	Isaias	Ida
Jose	Joyce	Jerry	Josephine	Joaquin
Katia	Kirk	Karen	Kyle	Kate
Lee	Leslie	Lorenzo	Laura	Larry
Maria	Michael	Melissa	Marco	Mindy
Nate	Madine	Nestor	Nana	Nicholas
Ophelia	Oscar	Olga	Omar	Odette
Philippe	Patty	Pablo	Paulette	Peter
Rina	Rafael	Rebekah	Rene	Rose
Sean	Sandy	Sebastien	Sally	Sam
Tammy	Tony	Tanya	Teddy	Teresa
Vince	Valerie	Van	Vicky	Victor
Whitney	William	Wendy	Wilfred	Wanda

Notable New England Hurricanes
Throughout History

Year	Dates	Name/Nickname
1635	08/25	Great Colonial Hurricane *
1638	08/03	Hurricane *(no known nickname)*
1675	09/07	Second Great Colonial Hurricane
1683	8/23	Hurricane and Flood of 1683
1713	08/30	Hurricane *(no known nickname)*
1727	09/27	Hurricane *(no known nickname)*
1743	11/02	Ben Franklin's Eclipse Hurricane
1749	10/19	Hurricane *(no known nickname)*
1761	10/23-24	Winthrop's Hurricane
1770	10/20	Stile's Hurricane
1778	08/12-13	The French Storm
1788	08/19	Western New England Hurricane
1815	09/23	The Great September Gale *
1821	09/03	Redfield's Hurricane *(came at low tide)*
1841	10/03	The October Gale
1856	08/21	Charter Oak Storm
1869	09/08	September Gale of '69
1878	10/23-24	Hurricane *(no known nickname)*
1879	08/18-19	Cape Cod Hurricane of '79
1893	08/24	Hurricane *(no known nickname)*
1893	08/29	*passed well inland*
1896	10/12-13	*offshore hurricane*
1916	07/21	*excessive rainfall*
1924	08/26	Offshore Hurricane of '24
1933	09/17-18	13.27 inches rain at Provincetown, MA
1936	09/18-19	7.79 inches rain at Provincetown, MA
1938	09/21	Great New England Hurricane *
1944	09/14-15	Great Atlantic Hurricane *
1950	09/11-12	Hurricane Dog
1954	08/31	Carol *
1954	09/11	Edna *
1955	08/17-19	Diane - *extreme flooding*
1960	09/12	Donna
1985	09/27	Gloria
1991	08/19	Bob

* Estimated at least a category 3 intensity on the Saffir-Simpson scale

Source: National Weather Service Boston

You be the Judge! ?

QUESTION: What do they name a hurricane if all the names on the list are used up?

A) It's named after the governor of the state where it makes landfall.

B) The Greek Alphabet is used.

C) It is named after famous meteorologists (where's Josh?).

ANSWER: B - The actual letters of the Greek alphabet are used, meaning the first three are: Alpha, Beta, Gamma

Wind Circulation and its Effects

Winds travel in a counter-clockwise rotation (in the northern hemisphere) spinning around the center of a hurricane. The middle is called the "eye." The strongest winds are usually found toward the center, right around the eye of the storm; this part is called the *eyewall*. Inside the eye is relative calm, where winds dissipate and often the sun comes out as it moves overhead. Many people have been fooled into thinking the storm was over, only to have the other side of the hurricane arrive.

The winds in a hurricane spin around the "eye" in a counter-clockwise rotation in the northern hemisphere and clockwise in the southern hemisphere.

In addition to the winds that circle around a tropical cyclone, the entire storm is also usually moving in a particular direction as well. This movement causes one side of the storm to be stronger and more dangerous than the other. The stronger side is the right side, in relation to the way the hurricane is traveling. Whichever way the storm is moving, from a bird's eye view, the right side would likely cause the most damage. This is because on the right, the winds circulating around are blowing in a motion that can be considered "forwards", and so when you combine that wind with the forward motion of the storm, the winds are actually even faster and stronger! (See illustration.) Therefore, if the winds swirling around a hurricane were 80 mph, and the storm was traveling at 20 mph, the winds on the right side of the storm would actually be 100 mph! The left side winds, however, would be 60 mph because the wind is blowing in the opposite direction that the storm is heading. Quite often, but not always, while the left side of the storm may be weaker, it produces heavier rainfall.

In addition to the faster wind speeds on the right, statistically there are also more tornadoes spawned and much higher *storm surge*.

Storm Surge: The biggest killer in hurricanes is flooding, usually as a result of storm surge. This can be described as a "wall of water" that is pushed ashore as the storm makes landfall.

HURRICANE MYTH: Storm surge is formed by a massive "suction" effect from low pressure in the eye. It picks water up and carries it with the hurricane.

HURRICANE FACT: Since the right side of a hurricane packs intense winds that blow forward while it travels, the wind pushes ocean water in a giant "mound." This bulge of water simply comes onto the land along with the storm, and can be 15 feet or higher and can wipe out structures and flood entire towns instantly. The matter is only worsened when hurricanes make landfall during high tide. Conversely, since the winds blow the opposite direction on the left side of a system, this side rarely has to deal with storm surge because water is being pushed away from land, although this side often receives heavier rainfall.

Hurricane Hunters

The 53rd Weather Reconnaissance Squadron is operated out of Keesler Air Force Base in Biloxi, Mississippi. They fly heavily constructed planes straight into hurricanes—on purpose! Their fleet is made up of ten Lockheed-Martin WC-120J aircraft. They are known as "The Hurricane Hunters," and they have been doing it since 1944.

As a storm is beginning to form, the National Hurricane Center activates these brave men and women to fly into it and investigate. The plane makes multiple passes through in a zig-zag fashion and drops several meteorological instruments to take readings. These tools help determine the exact center of the storm, wind speeds, pressure, and other important data that is imperative for tracking the system. In fact, with this information, the National Hurricane Center is able to forecast hurricanes an average of 30% better than without. When storms are active, the planes fly missions up to twice a day to get the most recent data they can.

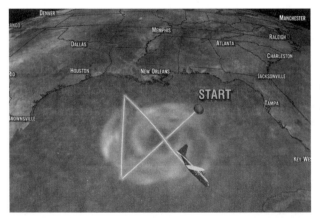

Also, quite often, Hurricane Hunter aircraft will drop a buoy in the ocean waters ahead of where a storm is heading, for future readings.

ABOVE: A typical flight path for a hurricane hunter aircrew.

RIGHT: The airplanes used to fly through hurricanes are built extra tough.

The Latest Information on Hurricanes

For up to date info, strength, and the projected track of any hurricane, go to the National Hurricane Center website, at: *www.nhc.noaa.gov.* You'll always find data and maps on any active hurricane or tropical storm, as well as predictions as to whether any are expected to form. You'll also find extensive archives of past storms, their intensity, and tracks.

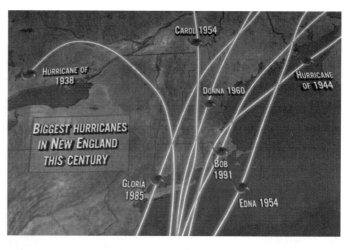

Notable Hurricanes and Stories

September 21, 1938: "The Great Hurricane of 1938"
(AKA "*The Great New England Hurricane*" and "*The Long Island Express*")

To this day, it remains the most powerful, costliest, and deadliest hurricane in New England history. At its peak a killer category 5, it made landfall on Long Island at category 3 status. Blue Hill Observatory, in Massachusetts, measured sustained winds of 121 mph with gusts to 186 mph. The absolute worst of it was felt in Rhode Island and eastern Connecticut, although much of New England experienced its mighty fury. At least 600 people were killed, over 700 were injured, and more than 57,000 homes were tattered or destroyed. Also of note, it's thought that over 25,000 automobiles were ruined and approximately 2 billion trees knocked down. Storm surge of at least 14 feet high struck coastal Rhode Island; and in Westerly it caused 100 deaths almost instantly.

Downtown Providence was washed out by storm surge during rush hour. Cars, trolleys, and everything else was under water.

Photo courtesy the Rhode Island Historical Society

Trees cover the streets of downtown Keene, NH, after the hurricane of 1938.

Photo courtesy Keene Public Library

Sitting on the beach in shock, a husband and wife in New Bedford taking in the damage.

Photo courtesy NOAA Photo Library

The Merrimack River in Manchester, NH, was in full flood.

Photo courtesy NOAA Photo Library

Kelley's Wharf in Fairhaven, MA, didn't survive the Great New England Hurricane.

Photo courtesy Spinner Publications
www.spinnerpub.com

Water everywhere in downtown Springfield, MA. The water made it difficult to transport sandbags.

Photo courtesy NOAA Photo Library

Island Park, RI was destroyed by a breaker reported to be 30 to 40 feet high.

Photo courtesy NOAA Photo Library

A boat is slammed into a tree in Mattapoisett, MA.

*Photo courtesy
Spinner Publications
www.spinnerpub.com*

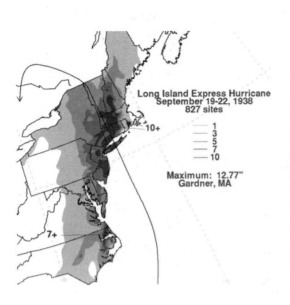

The track and rainfall amounts from the Hurricane of 1938.

Flooding in downtown Hartford from the hurricane of 1938. The Music Shell in Bushnell Park wasn't able to host any concerts for a while after it turned into a lake.

Photo courtesy NOAA Photo Library

eXtreme Weather eXtra!

Don Kent's Hurricane of '38 Memories

A never-before-published interview with the late New England forecasting legend Don Kent (1917 - 2010), conducted by New Hampshire author Eric Pinder in 2005, about Don's memories of the hurricane of '38.

"I was twenty years old at the time," remembers Don Kent. "It was the morning of September 21. I was at a little radio station in Boston, working for nothing. I didn't even get my carfare going from downtown Boston out to Kenmore Square." Early that morning he looked at the weather map and saw trouble. "I actually talked about a 1938 hurricane at noon that day and told everyone to go home and take their boats out of the water. I said, 'I'm brand new at this thing, but I've never seen such a tremendous storm moving so fast.'" The Weather Bureau--precursor to today's National Weather Service--did not agree. They only issued a Northeast storm warning and predicted gales of up to 40 mph.

"My witnesses to that are all dead now, unfortunately," says Kent. "But there was a cop in the corner of the street there where I worked. So I told him about it. I said, 'I'm going to rush home, take care of my boat because by five o'clock things are really going to pieces here. I've never seen anything so big.' But I didn't use the word hurricane, because there hadn't been a hurricane for one hundred fifteen years."

The policeman heeded his warning. Says Kent with a laugh, "So for the next twenty years or so, whenever I was around Boston, I could park on Chauncey Street in downtown Boston, free. He'd take care of it! Because I saved his boat, too!"

The damage was staggering. "We lost power for a week and the National Guard stood watch over the destruction," remembers Don Kent. "That day gave me a new perspective on the fickle nature of New England weather. The day before was beautiful and just hours later followed the worst storm of the century."

Distant Rhode Island Memories from '38

By Joel Feinberg

It's amazing how certain events can remain in your memory bank. I was four years old in 1938 when we had the Great Hurricane of September 1938. In those days there was very little warning of an approaching storm. The storm crossed Long Island and then took dead aim at Rhode Island. It went right up Narragansett Bay and into downtown Providence. It came in with the tide and as a result, downtown Providence was totally flooded. (They have since constructed a hurricane barrier, and this has stopped future storms from riding up the bay into Providence.)

My Grandmother and aunt were in downtown Providence shopping. The storm surge happened in late afternoon, and the water rose ten feet or more in all the department stores. People were stranded for two days on the top floors of these stores. I recall my uncle swimming through the water to get into one of the department stores to see if my aunt was OK.

I also can remember sitting in my living room, near Brown University, on the East side of Providence watching every tree on the north side of my street blow over. For some reason those trees on the south side of the street survived!

It was a monster storm. Stories of people surviving it were told for years to come. My grandfather used to tell me of the NYC Blizzard of 1888. So in my family, we added the 1938 hurricane, and then the local blizzard of 1978, right up there with weather events to never forget!

The Great Atlantic Hurricane of 1944 - September 15, 1944: A storm of this magnitude, just six years after the 1938 hurricane, was not what the people in our region wanted. This cyclone was a bit farther east, making landfall from the south near the Rhode Island/Connecticut border. Then it headed right over Boston and from there went back out to sea. As it traveled up the Gulf of Maine it skimmed along the coast of that state as well, as it accelerated toward Nova Scotia. Hurricane force winds were felt in many parts of New England, including a 109 mph gust recorded in Hartford, Connecticut. Up to eleven inches of rain fell in parts of New England. A total of 390 people died from the storm, 26 of which were from New England. In Maine, one of those fatalities was caused when a bicyclist was blinded by heavy rain and ran over a 40-year old woman.

An aerial picture shows the wreckage from the 1944 hurricane in Edgartown, MA, on Martha's Vineyard.

Photo courtesy Spinner Publications
www.spinnerpub.com

Trees knocked over onto house after house in Mattapoisett, MA.

Photo courtesy Spinner Publications

www.spinnerpub.com

More damage caused by the hurricane near the Centerville – Osterville Bridge on Cape Cod.
Photo courtesy Spinner Publications | www.spinnerpub.com

The "Mary M." fishing vessel sinks at Union Wharf in Fairhaven, MA unable to withstand the hurricane.
Photo courtesy Spinner Publications | www.spinnerpub.com

Flooding on Craigville Beach in Hyannis, MA.
Photo courtesy Spinner Publications | www.spinnerpub.com

The 1944 hurricane brought down the radio transmitting tower for WOCB radio in West Yarmouth.
It also toppled the radio tower for WNBH in New Bedford (not shown).
Photo courtesy Spinner Publications | www.spinnerpub.com

August 30, 1954 - Carol: As many hurricanes do, Carol made landfall over Long Island and then moved over Connecticut as it steamed northward. Southern Connecticut and Rhode Island absorbed a direct hit, with storm surge of 10 to 15 feet and wind gusts of 110 mph. The most affected communities to deal with this devastation were New London and points eastward, such as Mystic and Groton, and right into Westerly and Charlestown, RI.

Hurricane Carol destroyed hundreds of homes in Westerly, Rhode Island.

Photo courtesy NOAA Photo Library

After landfall, it quickly began weakening over western Massachusetts, and lost even more of its punch when moving over southern Vermont and New Hampshire, although it was still powerful. In total, wind and storm surge demolished 4,000 homes, 3,500 cars, and over 3,000 boats. At one point, 85% of all Connecticut had lost its electricity, as well as large portions of Rhode Island and Massachusetts. In Boston, the spire of the Old North Church was blown down. Storm surge in Massachusetts, amongst other damage, transported salt water into forests, which killed thousands of trees. Another casualty were crops: apple, corn, peach, and tomato crops from almost every state in New England were damaged to the tune of millions of dollars. Although it lost some of its punch farther north, the winds were still strong enough to destroy part of Canobie Lake Park's "Yankee Cannonball" roller coaster track, in Salem, NH.

Storm surge from Carol washes right into the Edgewood Yacht Club in Rhode Island.

Photo courtesy NOAA Photo Library

An amazing picture of the storm surge coming in during Hurricane Carol.

Photo courtesy Spinner Publications www.spinnerpub.com

New Bedford, MA: Thousands of boats were washed ashore, destroyed, and piled up after Carol.

Photo courtesy Spinner Publications www.spinnerpub.com

September 11, 1954 - Edna: It was almost unimaginable; Edna struck New England just under two weeks after Carol. Luckily this second storm wasn't quite as intense and was farther east, but it still caused a lot of problems. Edna was also responsible for 21 deaths in the region, 12 of which were here in New England.

The storm struck Martha's Vineyard and Nantucket, as well as the far eastern tip of Cape Cod, bringing winds over 100 mph. Providence reported winds to 90 mph and Boston a saw a brief gust to 101 mph! Power was wiped out on nearly all of the Cape, as well as eastern Massachusetts and Rhode Island. From there, Edna made a beeline to the Maine coast where it would wreak even more havoc. Edna brought wind gusts of up to 74 mph to the Pine Tree state. Storm surge and wind damage along the coast was tremendous, and rainfall amounts were between seven and eight inches. The heavy rains sent rivers gushing over their banks and washing out roads and bridges. Eight people died in Maine alone, all due to drowning. Many Mainers consider Edna to be Maine's worst-ever hurricane.

Swampscott, MA: A car is crushed by a large tree. Edna's wind was strong enough to topple very large trees.

Photo from the collection of John Milleker, Ipswitch, Mass.

Hurricane Edna brought destruction to the Salisbury, MA, Drive-in Theatre.

Photo from the collection of John Milleker Ipswich, Mass.

August 19, 1955 – Diane: By the time Diane made it to New England, it had been downgraded to a tropical storm after making landfall in North Carolina. The storm's biggest effect on New England was extreme flooding as it brought heavy rainfall of 10 to 15 inches on average. The highest rain amounts were found in Massachusetts and northern parts of Connecticut and Rhode Island. Westfield, MA, set the all-time rainfall record for New England (for one storm) with 19.75" collected, a record which still stands today. Some of the damaged structures were still in the rebuilding process from the two hurricanes the year before. The three northern New England states escaped with little or no rain whatsoever.

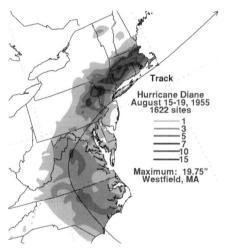

Track

Hurricane Diane
August 15-19, 1955
1622 sites

——— 1
——— 3
——— 5
——— 7
——— 10
——— 15

Maximum: 19.75"
Westfield, MA

Extreme flooding in Waterbury, Connecticut after Diane.
Photo courtesy NOAA Photo Library.

September 12, 1960 – Donna: One of the most remarkable things about Donna is that the hurricane traveled up the entire east coast of the United States. In fact, Donna is the only hurricane on record to produce hurricane force winds in Florida, the Mid-Atlantic States, and New England! Donna hit New England as a category 2 storm, reaching southeast Connecticut with sustained winds of 100 mph, gusting to 125-130 mph, cutting diagonally through the region to Maine. Block Island reported sustained winds of 95 mph and gusts to 130 mph and the Blue Hill Observatory charted gusts to 145 mph. The storm produced pockets of 4-8" rainfall amounts and storm surge five to ten feet high. There were three fatalities in New England, all in Massachusetts.

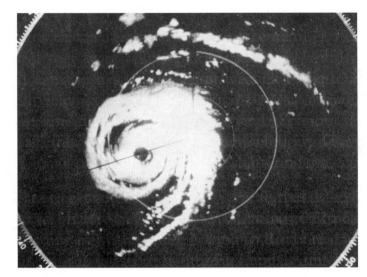

RDU
HIGHWAY PATROL RPT FROM ILM WEATHER BUREAU SAYS THAT EYE WAS OVER
STATION AT 0225Z
WINDS GUSTING TO 91MPH AT 0130Z
ABV RECEIVED BY FONE AT RDU

STATEMENT ON HURRICANE DONNA ISSUED BY BOSTON WEATHER BUREAU
10PM EDT SEPTEMBER 11 1960

HURRICANE WATCH IN EFFECT 10 PM EDT NORTH OF PORTSMOUTH TO EASTPORT.
HURRICANE WARNINGS ARE NOW DISPLAYED FROM BLOCK ISLAND TO PORTSMOUTH
NEW HAMPSHIRE AND GALE WARNINGS NORTH OF PORTSMOUTH TO EASTPORT.

HURRICANE DONNA IS ACCELERATING RAPIDLY AS SHE MOVES
NORTHEASTWARD ALONG THE MIDDLE ATLANTIC COAST AND ITS NOW IMPERATIVE THAT
PRECAUTIONS AGAINST HURRICANE FORCE WINDS AND ABNORMALLY HIGH TIDES
BE TAKEN BEFORE DAYBREAK OVER RHODE ISLAND EASTERN MASS
AND CAPE COD.

EAST TO NORTHEAST WINDS WILL BEGIN TO INCREASE ALONG THE
RHODE ISLAND AND MASS COASTS DURING THE EARLY MORNING HOURS ON
MONDAY PROBABLY REACHING HURRICANE FORCE BY MID MORNING.
WINDS WILL REACH GALE FORCE ALONG THE NEW HAMPSHIRE AND MAINE COASTS BY
MID DAY MONDAY.

FURTHER DETAILS ON THE PROGRESS OF THIS DANGEROUS
HURRICANE WILL BE ISSUED AT FREQUENT INTERVALS DURING THE
NIGHT. KEEP TURNED TO LOCAL RADIO OR TELEVISION STATION.

DREBERT WEATHER BUREAU BOSTON

A weather statement issued by the Boston Weather Bureau as Donna approached the area.

ABOVE: A radar image of Hurricane Donna. Radar was very new and this was one of the first few hurricanes ever studied with it.

LEFT: A child plays in the flooded road in New Bedford, after Hurricane Donna moves through.

Photo courtesy Spinner Publications
www.spinnerpub.com

September 27, 1985 Gloria: It had been 25 years since the last hurricane (Donna) had made a track through New England. As most do in this region, Gloria approached from the south and made landfall over Long Island and then through southern Connecticut, from there heading north-northeast through Massachusetts and on to New Hampshire and Maine. Vermont incurred the least effects of the storm, with just rain and a few reports of flooding.

As the hurricane struck southern New England as a category 1 storm, powerful winds brought down trees and ripped roofs off of buildings. Since the storm made landfall during low tide, Connecticut, Massachusetts and Rhode Island received a lot less flooding from the storm surge, which was limited to five feet or less. In general, the consensus afterwards was that Gloria did not pack as much of a punch as was expected, despite widespread damage. As with most hurricanes, there were a lot of people who lost power from the storm, amounting to approximately 1.2 million outages in New England. New Hampshire and Vermont had the fewest power failures, but they did receive between three and six inches of rain that fell in short periods of time, causing some minor flooding. Seven deaths can be directly attributed to Gloria, four of them in Massachusetts, most of which were caused by falling tree limbs.

One thing that many New Englanders remember about that storm was the masking tape that was put on windows in buildings practically everywhere! It was quite a sight to see the masking tape in virtually every single window; some people turned it into an art form. At the time, this advice was given because it was thought the practice would stop windows from blowing out.

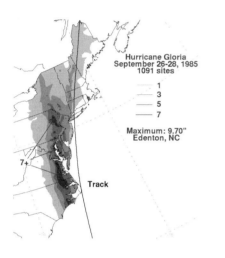

Hurricane Gloria
September 26-28, 1985
1091 sites

— 1
— 3
— 5
— 7

Maximum: 9.70"
Edenton, NC

Track

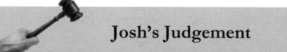

Josh's Judgement

According to the National Hurricane Center, recent research has shown that putting tape on your windows before a hurricane arrives is a waste of time, effort, and tape. It does not stop windows from shattering or stop pieces of glass from flying across a room. You should either stay far away from windows, or put wooden boards over the windows instead.

The following three pictures show New Bedford, Massachusetts right after Gloria barreled through.
Photos by Timothy C. Bayer

TOP RIGHT: Trees blocking Rounds Street after Gloria's wind took them down.

BOTTOM RIGHT: Note the masking tape X in the window, and the wires down in the yard.

MIDDLE: This car's owner had parked far away from the trees hoping to avoid damage. Who would have known a chimney would collapse and fall on the car!

Tough Tractor Trailer Trips during Gloria!

By Eunice Miller

MY STORY

SURVIVING EXTREME WEATHER

I remember hearing that a storm would arrive with hurricane force winds and they were telling us on the news pretty much to batten down the hatches. Well I lived in a second-floor apartment in Salem, NH, so with the large glass windows I set about using masking tape and made a large X on each window. They said this would help to keep the glass from shattering into very small pieces.

With that done I had to get some sleep as my days started at 2:30 AM. I owned my own tractor (as in semi truck) and I had to be in Roxbury, MA for my first load by 4 AM. Well, after getting to Roxbury and loading up with the city's rubbish, I was told my load was to go down to the Cape. After I pumped off my load of rubbish in a landfill, I headed back north to go pick up load #2. I did this all day with the winds kicking up with each passing hour. I hit headwinds going south and tail winds going back into Roxbury; it was a pretty interesting driving day. I had a fabric cover on top of the rubbish and it really could not do what it was designed to do. With the 50+ mph winds, trash was coming out of trailer and no matter what I did I could not fix the problem.

I lost my cover on load #3 and a Mass State Trooper stopped to ask if I was OK. I told him I was sorry for the mess on the road and he said "be careful," and left, no fine! So now the day is coming to an end and I start to "bobtail" home to New Hampshire. I get up to the old split on I-93 North/Tobin Bridge, where there was another trooper who stopped me and said the road was shut down. I told him I had to get home to New Hampshire and he said they shut the Tobin down due to winds. I laughed and said "My lucky day." Off I went to my taped- up apartment, where the winds never got bad, but I spent a long time getting that tape off!

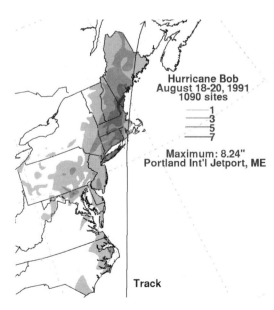

Hurricane Bob
August 18-20, 1991
1090 sites

1
3
5
7

Maximum: 8.24"
Portland Int'l Jetport, ME

Track

August 19, 1991 Bob: Hurricane Bob made landfall over Block Island and then Newport, RI, in the afternoon as a category 2 on the Saffir-Simpson Scale, with winds measuring 100 mph. Storm surge in Narragansett Bay was 11.5 feet high, and parts of Buzzard's Bay received 12 to 15 foot surges. Interestingly, it was the only hurricane to make a U.S. landfall during that 1991 season. Winds were the strongest over Rhode Island and eastern Massachusetts, where over 60% of those residents lost their power. Hurricane force winds were felt in most areas east of the Connecticut River. Bob quickly weakened to a category 1 storm while over southeastern Massachusetts, with the eye moving between Boston and Scituate. Along the way, there were two unconfirmed reports of tornadoes in Rhode Island, as well as two reports in Massachusetts. Then Bob returned to the ocean just south of Boston, and made a second landfall as a tropical storm near Rockland, Maine and proceeded up toward Canada. Maine's top winds clocked in at 61 mph, which still were enough to knock out power and topple thousands of trees.

Over 2 million homes and businesses lost electricity, some for over a week. President George H.W. Bush declared Rhode Island a disaster area due to the widespread destruction. Along the track of the storm, rainfall amounts of five to eight inches were common. Bob was responsible for eighteen deaths in the United States, six of which were in Connecticut and three in Maine.

LEFT: Homes beyond repair in Wareham, Massachusetts, thanks to Hurricane Bob.
Photo by Michael Coughlin

RIGHT: The Atlantic churns up in Maine at Pemaquid Point, as Hurricane Bob nears.
Photo by Kathy Davis

Hurricane Bob August 20-21, 1991

Meteorologist Bob Maxon, NBC Connecticut, Hartford, CT

As a 26-year-old, weekday meteorologist working (at the time) at WMUR-TV, my youthful exuberance would lead to road trips almost every weekend. Coastal Maine, hiking in the Green or Whites, fun around Fenway and Faneuil Hall, or racing to Newport, RI, to spend time with friends. I had very few responsibilities in my life. I came and went as I pleased.

The weekend of August 18th and 19th in 1991 was highlighted by the marriage of my great friend Frank Mallicoat (of FOX 25) to his wife, Monique. It was a Sunday ceremony on the North Shore of Massachusetts, which meant a quick turnaround into Monday morning television news. The big subject at the reception was the pending hurricane and how its arrival might delay the new couple's flight to their honeymoon destination. Not whether evacuations were needed, or if boats should be brought to dry-dock or at least tightened on their moorings. No discussions about hurricane preparations as Bob was expected to give Cape Cod a solid hit, but do little as far as damage to New Hampshire or the North Shore. Several inches of rain were expected, and some wind—but that type of weather happened quite often in New England as the well-known "nor'easter."

While the wedding reception was winding down in Revere, MA, hurricane coverage planning was underway in the newsroom at WMUR-TV. The planning was tempered by a separate weather-related tragedy that needed coverage. While the hurricane loomed off the Carolina coastline that night, our coverage centered on how a microburst had killed five and injured eleven in Stratham, NH. The thick, moisture-laden air mass in advance of Bob fueled the microburst that knocked over a picnic shelter where a family sought shelter. It was an eye-opener that the atmosphere was really juiced, and some amazing conditions were possible as Bob crept ever closer.

I spent the predawn hours analyzing the track of the hurricane while attempting to forecast its impact on New Hampshire. A state with 19 miles of seacoast seems to have a keen attachment to that area as one of its crown jewels due to its natural beauty. But most of the population is concentrated inland, along the Nashua-Salem-Manchester-Concord corridor. My forecast had to reflect how the storm would impact *our* people, *our* roads, and *our* rivers and streams, while resisting the temptation to detail how Bob would slam Cape Cod and Rhode Island. I detailed my thoughts that too much rain would fall in a short period of time inland, while a period of strong gusty winds would buffet our seacoast. Emergency managers and local government officials prepared for power outages, tree damage, beach erosion and some minor structural damage to beach homes on the Atlantic Ocean.

Right after ABC's *Good Morning America* ended, the decision was made to send me to Hampton Beach, NH, and file live reports as we expected to start wall-to-wall coverage of the hurricane as it rolled by to our east. In 1991, interrupting the normal daytime television schedule for weather coverage was quite rare and left for only the biggest weather events, so I found a needed second wind as I neared Ocean Blvd. and helped set up a live broadcast site. When anchor Karen Appel opened our noon newscast that day it started six-plus hours of live coverage as Bob roared by. Our team of meteorologists included Rick Gordon in studio and Mish Michaels in the weather center relaying extreme weather information to me in the field. Looking back, I realize this was an amazing feat. There was no Internet. Cell phones were big and expensive with spotty service, and text messaging, Twitter, or social networking was almost 20 years in the future! Mish would communicate current weather conditions to me via two-way radio and I would report how it looked and felt on the Seacoast. The coverage continued through "Live at 5" and our 6:00 PM newscast was interrupted only by a few reports for WCVB in Boston and a new cable news channel called "CNN!"

In the end, the storm gave us memorable graze, highlighted by three to six inches of rain and wind that gusted to near 70 mph., thousands left without power, and unfortunately two people dead. The thing I remember most from that day was the television coverage. It was thorough without hype, long in duration without being too repetitious, and informative as it guided viewers through a near-catastrophic storm. The statistics mean little to me 19 years later; instead, I remember learning that day the importance of my job as a broadcast meteorologist, working as a forecaster, reporter and guide to the viewers as they experience such a significant storm.

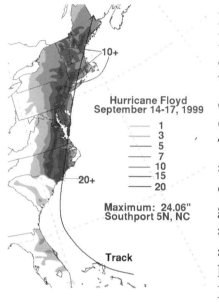

Floyd - September 17, 1999: Although it was once a category 4 hurricane, by the time Floyd made it to New England, it had been downgraded to a tropical storm, with top winds of 50 to 60 mph. While over Maine, it lost all tropical characteristics and was downgraded to an extratropical storm. Floyd made landfall over Cape Fear, North Carolina and then accelerated up the east coast. The biggest problem Floyd brought to our area was heavy rain and power outages. Much of New England calculated four to eight inches of rain, with a few spots in Connecticut and Vermont getting up to 10 inches. Danbury, CT received top prize, with almost 15 inches, which led to major flooding problems in and around the city. Around New England, flooding covered hundreds of local roads and caused them to be closed for days. Mudslides were even reported in the Berkshire region of western Massachusetts. Luckily, since New England had been in a drought before the storm, the flood waters were absorbed into the dry ground rather quickly.

Satellite imagery of Floyd, while it was off the coast of Florida and before it raced toward New England.

Photo courtesy NOAA

Hurricane Floyd memories – Cruising for Trouble

Meteorologist Josh Judge – WMUR TV, New Hampshire

Hurricane Floyd is very memorable for me because my wife and I were on a cruise ship to Bermuda, and Floyd was steaming through the Atlantic Ocean. We boarded the cruise at Boston's Black Falcon Terminal and began the journey south. At this time, the hurricane was down near the Bahamas and was churning up the seas all the way up and down the Atlantic. Now, this was my first cruise and I was nervous about how choppy the ride would be, but was advised "not to worry, the stabilizers will keep the boat pretty calm."

Once we got underway, it quickly became apparent to me that this would not be the case. Although I grew up around many smaller boats, I had never been seasick in my life. That changed on this cruise. I'm sure that taking a cruise is fantastic 99.8% of the time, but this was perhaps one of those voyages which belong in that last .2%. I felt trapped for the entire three-day trip to Bermuda, like a sardine locked in a can. Up and down, over and over, it felt like it would never end. I still have vivid memories of seeking out a big open hallway so I could lie down, only to find that several dozen other people had the same idea, and clogged the hallway. No matter, I couldn't walk any farther, and I quickly joined them for while until I had the energy to return to my rocky cabin.

By the time we got to Bermuda, I was so happy to set foot on dry and stable land! We had a fantastic time while there, although even when in my bed at the hotel, it still felt like the whole room was swaying back and forth. During our stay, hurricane Floyd made landfall in the Carolinas and began its path up the East Coast. The idea that we would have to take the cruise ship back to Boston after the hurricane had further chopped up the waters was terrifying to me.

Finally, that day came that we were in the shuttle van and headed back to the ship. We met another couple on the way there who gave us some extra seasick patches they had. We put them behind our ears and prayed they would help on the bumpy ride home. Would you believe it? They did! The trip back was even rockier than the way down, but the medicine worked, and I never felt sick. I learned two lessons on that trip: One, stay away from hurricanes on cruises. Two, always make a trip to your doctor beforehand and get some seasickness medication to take with you.

ABOVE: This building in Fairhaven, MA and its surroundings were also no match for The Great Hurricane of '38. *Photo courtesy Spinner Publications | www.spinnerpub.com*

BELOW: Rough seas from Edna in Nahant, MA. *Photo from the collection of John Milleker Ipswich MA*

Salisbury, Vermont: A flash flood has washed part of the road away. Vermont Governor Jim Douglas walks
across to survey the damage. *Photo by Barbara Farr, Vermont Emergency Management*

CHAPTER 9: FLOODING

Flooding may not come to mind quite as fast as other disasters, but believe it or not, it accounts for more weather related deaths than lightning or even tornadoes! In fact, when you combine the different types of flooding, it is the biggest weather-related killer, not to mention the extensive monetary damage it causes.

Most often, floods occur because of too much rain. Either the rain falls too fast for the ground, drainage systems and rivers to keep up, or it falls for a long duration and gradually over-saturates the ground. There can be other reasons, either in combination with high rainfalls or by themselves. For example, a dam break can cause flooding devastation, which may or may not be caused by heavy rains.

In the springtime, snow melt adds to the problems. When the snow melts slowly there isn't usually a problem, but when heavy rain forces the melting and adds to it, big trouble can follow. Also during the spring and fall seasons, severe flooding often happens when a coastal storm or nor'easter moves over and stalls nearby. Often times, a front settles overhead and transfers water from the ocean into copious amounts of rainfall. During the warm season, thunderstorms can create deluging downpours which drop several inches of rain in a very short time span.

There are different types of floods. Let's define them:

River Floods

This type of flood occurs when a river swells up and overflows its banks. Most often, it happens after heavy amounts of rain, snowmelt, an ice jam, or a combination of any of the three. This is the most frequent type of flooding we deal with here in the northeast.

People who live near rivers are especially prone to floods and must monitor forecasts when flooding is possible. River gauges monitor many of the larger rivers around New England and can give forecasters early warning when the risk is growing for a river to brim over. These gauges automatically record the water level and relay the

The Ipswich River in North Andover, Massachusetts, rises above its banks.
Photo by Bruce Aspeslagh

information to those who specialize in river forecasts. You can view river levels in real-time by visiting this website, *www.weather.gov/ahps* and then clicking on your region of the country, then the river of your choice. Knowing the level of a river can give you a heads up of whether flooding may be getting closer. The website also shows you computer predictions of what the river may do in the future.

FLOOD MYTH: Big vehicles and SUV's are safe to drive through flooded roads.

FLOOD FACT: It only takes two feet of water to float almost any vehicle. If the water is moving, your car can be swept away! Almost half of all flood related deaths happen inside vehicles.

Flash Floods

These are the most dangerous kind of floods, because they happen very quickly and sometimes without warning. In these scenarios, water rises quite fast due to very heavy rain, overflowing rivers or dam bursts, ice jams, rapid snowmelt, or levee failure, just to name a few reasons. Often they occur either near a river or in urban areas with poor drainage. Flash floods can also occur after heavy rains run down the sides of hills and overwhelm the areas below.

Providence, Rhode Island: The way this piece of playground equipment sticks out of the water, it looks like some sort of sea creature.
Photo by Caitlin Mahoney

The water moves with such force that anything in its path can be wiped out or washed away, including boulders, trees, and even buildings.

Flash floods can happen during almost any time of year. They're common in the spring and fall when nor'easters and other systems (like hurricanes and tropical storms) bring huge amounts of rain very quickly. In the winter, ice that forms on rivers can dislodge and then get jammed as it rounds corners or passes under bridges, which slows the flow of water and floods the upstream areas. Finally, flash floods are quite common in the warmer months, with the catalyst being thunderstorms which can produce a lot of rain in a very short time.

FLASH FLOOD MYTH: Flash floods only happen when it's raining.

FLASH FLOOD FACT: There only needs to be rain falling upstream if you are along a river.

FLOODING MYTH: A "100-year Flood" only happens once every one hundred years.

FLOODING FACT: Just because of its name, doesn't mean they only happen once a century! In fact, there have been 100-year floods that took place two years in a row. The meaning of the term is simply that there's a 1% chance of a major and unusual flood in any area every year.

Coastal Floods

Waves crash over a sea wall and flood the area.
Photo by the Associated Press.

This type of flooding most often occurs along with storm systems that move though, especially those over the ocean. As the strong winds circulate around ocean storms and gales, the wind also pushes water in somewhat the same way hurricanes create storm surge. When these winds blow the water toward land, it can cause coastal flooding as water comes ashore. At times of high tide, the wind can blow the water even farther inland because of the higher water levels. Even if the storm isn't a blockbuster, combine the storm and high tide, and there may be flooding. Add in a near full moon or new moon, and you've an *astronomical* high tide, and you've got the potential for damaging coastal flooding.

Urban Flooding

Bigger towns and cities usually have much more concrete and pavement, and less soil to absorb rain water. After heavy rains, all the water runs off and must go down municipal drainage systems. Because of the vast amounts of water, sometimes they just can't handle it fast enough and water backs up into the streets or worse, into buildings. The good news is that although urban flooding can be very costly, there are rarely fatalities involved.

Water runs across Route 28 in Salem, New Hampshire.

Photo by Dave Peatfield, courtesy Ulocal.wmur.com

More Facts About Flooding

• Flash flooding after torrential rainfall is the number one cause of deaths from thunderstorms (not lightning as you might think).

• Most deaths from flash flooding happen at night and are of people who become trapped in their vehicle.

• As mentioned above, two feet of water will cause almost any vehicle to float. Just six inches can knock a person off their feet.

ABOVE: A parking lot fills with water at Keene State College in New Hampshire after the floods of October 2005.

Photo courtesy NH Homeland Security and Emergency Management.

LEFT: Flash flooding covers a street in Meredith, NH. It is extremely dangerous to drive through flooded roadways.

ABOVE: Flash Flooding was strong enough to rip apart this road in Newfields, NH.

Photo courtesy Ulocal.wmur.com

RIGHT: Connecticut, March 2010: It's not highly recommended that you use these stairs right now.

Photo by Dave Gilbert

Notable Flooding and Stories

The New England Flood of November, 1927: When a late season hurricane moved up the east coast, it brought torrential downpours to the northeast. It had already been an above average fall season for rain, so the ground was saturated. Hardest hit was Vermont, with western parts of Massachusetts and New Hampshire also racking up high totals. Widespread six to ten inch amounts were common, with isolated areas seeing up to 15". Some of the worst flooding was found in Vermont along the Winooski River, which ended up flooding most of downtown Montpelier under eight to ten feet of water. Hundreds were left homeless in the Green Mountain State and many small towns were

In 1927, the water ran into the streets of downtown Keene, New Hampshire.

Photo courtesy Keene Public Library

abandoned for weeks, as they were uninhabitable. The storm took 85 lives, of which 84 were residents of Vermont. Also affected were: the Connecticut and White Rivers, the Pemigewasset River through New Hampshire, and the Merrimack River from the Granite State down into Lowell, Massachusetts.

Amazing picture of the devastating flooding in Nashua, New Hampshire in 1936. Photo from the "Report on the 1936 Flood" by the New Hampshire Flood Reconstruction Council.

March 1936 – The "All New England Flood": With a deep snow pack in place, up to 20 inches of monsoon-like rainfall and warm temperatures, rapid melting followed. Rivers and streams spilled over while landslides and avalanches caused major damage. An astounding 50,000 families were displaced from their homes. Major cities were submerged, including: Manchester and Nashua, NH; Lowell, Lawrence, and Haverhill, MA; Hartford, CT.

Water from the Merrimack River spills into downtown Lawrence, Massachusetts. *Photos courtesy Bruce Aspeslagh*

LEFT: Flooding in downtown Keene, NH, after the floods of 1936. *Photo courtesy Keene Public Library*

RIGHT: An ice jam in Maine. When ice jams, it can lead to extensive flooding.
Photo courtesy National Weather Service Caribou, ME.

March 17-19, 1968: Although not as widespread as some other flood events, this one impacted the heavily populated areas of eastern Massachusetts and the northern half of Rhode Island. A rain storm moved in over ground already saturated from a previous storm and dropped up to seven inches of rain on areas from Boston down to Providence. The highest flood stages were seen on the Charles, Ipswich, Blackstone, Neponset, and Taunton Rivers, among others.

The 1968 flooding was localized to areas south of Boston along the coast and in northern Rhode Island.
Image courtesy The Northeast River Forecast Center

April 1, 1987 – Maine flooding: Many homes and businesses along Maine's major waterways were swept away, along with roads and bridges. An average of four to six inches of rainfall combined with over six feet of melting snow and frozen ground, producing severe flooding. The worst of it was along the Kennebec River, which rose to historic levels, washing out roads and bridges, and flooding over 2,000 homes and 400 businesses. At least two historic structures were also leveled. The town of Waterville lived up to its name, as most of the area was underneath five feet of water!

The Kennebec River in Maine overflows its banks in 1987.
Photo courtesy The River Forecast Center

Sandbags at the ready at the Green Line subway's Kenmore Square station in Boston.

Photo courtesy Mass. DOT

October 20-21, 1996: A powerful nor'easter moved through, tapping moisture from a distant hurricane Lili, and depositing huge amounts of rain on much of New England from Maine to Boston and beyond. Rainfall amounts of five to ten inches were common in parts of Massachusetts, New Hampshire, and Maine. Lesser amounts of two to four inches fell in Rhode Island, Connecticut, and Vermont. In southern Maine, an astounding 19.21" of water fell in Saco, nearly setting a new all-time New England storm rainfall record. (The record is 19.76" which fell during Hurricane Diane in 1955 in Westfield, MA.) In Boston, an offshoot of the Charles River overflowed into the Green Line subway system at Kenmore Square, filling it up with over 20 feet of water. The system was knocked out of service for several days. The water also washed out well over a mile of track and partially flooded five other subway stations. As with other major floods, hundreds of roadways were under water and 81 bridges needed to be rebuilt afterwards.

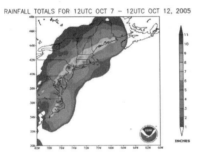

A summary of the rain totals from October 7-12, 2005.
Photo courtesy NOAA

October 8-9, 2005: The rain came down hard with the highest tallies in western parts of Connecticut and Massachusetts, as well as Cheshire County in southwestern New Hampshire. As much as eleven inches of rain collected in some localized areas. Alstead, NH, was among the hardest hit, after a dam break sent a surge of water down the Cold River. Bridges and roads were wiped out for miles, a four-mile stretch of Route 123 buckled, and all roads to and from the town were closed. The flooding killed seven people, four of whom were residents of Alstead. Many homes were completely demolished; even the town's police station flooded almost to the ceiling. Over one thousand people were evacuated from their homes in the area, and surrounding towns along the river suffered heavy damage as well. Nearby Keene was 30 to 40 percent under water and National Guard units were deployed to assist with evacuations.

In western Massachusetts, extreme flooding for some farmers meant that their fields flooded. This is notable, because it was early October and the fields were filled with pumpkins, many of which floated away! People in these areas still refer to it to this day as "The Pumpkin Flood."

Water flooded many fields in western Massachusetts and hundreds of pumpkins floated away.
Photo courtesy Derek Maroot of Northeast Kingdom Weather

ABOVE: An entire neighborhood in Keene, New Hampshire is flooded during the floods of October 2005.

BELOW: Route 9 in Sullivan, New Hampshire is completely wiped out.

Photos courtesy NH Homeland Security and Emergency Management

Devastating damage, as seen from the state police helicopter over Rt. 123 between Alstead and Walpole, NH.

Photos courtesy NH Homeland Security and Emergency Management

ABOVE: A parking lot full of water in Keene. And you thought you had problems parking?

BELOW: A road in Keene, NH, washed away.

ABOVE: Keene, NH October 2005: After the October 2005 flooding, this soccer field's goal was to dry up.

BELOW: When you bring your car into the shop, you expect it to be fixed, not flooded.

Photos courtesy NH Homeland Security and Emergency Management

Watch out for that first step! An Alstead, NH house with all the surroundings washed away. As a coincidence, this was an Alstead firefighter's home, so perhaps he's used to climbing on ladders.

RIGHT: A house along Route 123 near Alstead. As emergency crews attempted to check for survivors or bodies, they spray painted their findings on the sides of houses, as seen here.

BELOW: The power of water. Cars and other large objects were tossed about and smashed during the flash flooding in Alstead.

Photos courtesy NH Homeland Security and Emergency Management

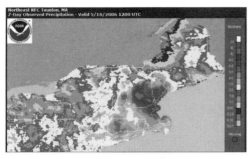

A map of the rainfall from the Mother's Day Floods of 2006. The highest rain amounts were in NH, southern Maine, and northeastern Massachusetts.

Image courtesy Northeast River Forecast Center

Mother's Day Floods of 2006: As an especially strong storm system stalled to our west, it drew in copious amounts of water from the Atlantic Ocean. At one time or another, virtually every county in New England was under a flood watch or warning. Rainfall amounts totaled 10-15" in the hardest hit areas, which were much of NH, southern Maine, and northeastern Massachusetts. Many homes and businesses in the areas with the highest totals reported the worst flooding since the hurricane of 1938. Rivers flooded over their banks, over one thousand roads were closed and/or washed away, and houses were evacuated. Among the worst hit was the Merrimack River, along with hundreds of other rivers, streams, and creeks.

North Reading, Massachusetts: One of the best ways to get around after the flood was by boat. *Photo courtesy Martins Pond Association*

A major problem for those affected by this storm was flooded basements. *Photo courtesy Martins Pond Association*

March 2010: Three separate nor'easters, each within a week of the other, deluged New England residents with one of the wettest months in history. In fact, it did set records for the wettest month ever from Providence up to the communities just southwest of Boston. Boston logged its second wettest month of all time and the wettest March ever. All three systems moved up the coast and stalled over the northeast, which kept the rain coming. Almost our entire region was affected, with rivers taking over towns and thousands of people evacuating their homes. Even areas with less rainfall faced flooding issues because the ground was still partially frozen, and therefore couldn't absorb water as effectively. Snowmelt had a hand in the problems as well, as it rushed down

ABOVE, RIGHT: Flooding in March 2010 knocked this Rhode Island radio station off the air, as water surrounded its broadcast tower. *Photo by Blair Harden*

Flooding takes over a large intersection in West Warwick, RI

Photo courtesy the Northeast River Forecast Center

the mountains and into rivers and streams. Since the storms were close together, the ground remained saturated and didn't have enough time to dry before the next system rolled in. Southern parts of New England suffered through the worst flooding, with the nastiest effects in Rhode Island, Connecticut, and southeastern Massachusetts. Rhode Island flooding was the worst in at least 200 years (possibly much more), almost completely flooding several towns as the Pawtuxet River rose to levels never seen in recorded history. Entire shopping malls and plazas were turned into lakes and hundreds of roads were covered. The damage was so bad that it prompted a visit from U.S. President Obama and several other top level officials.

Strong winds were also a factor in one of the storms, with top gusts in northern New England to 50+ mph, which knocked a tree across Rte. I-93 in New Hampshire, killing a motorist. Southern New England saw even stronger winds, with Norwalk, CT, registering a gust of 65 mph and East Milton, MA, reporting 69 mph.

ABOVE: The rainstorm brought new meaning to this town's name: Watertown, Massachusetts. Water from the Charles River spilled over its banks after days of rain.

Photo by Sean Graham

RIGHT: A streetlight reflects off the flood waters in Rocky Hill, Connecticut.

Photo by Dave Gilbert

Norwood Airport, Massachusetts: "Attention passengers, your flight may be a bit delayed."

Photo courtesy Mass. DOT

ABOVE: This is usually a busy area of West Warwick, Rhode Island. Flooding put the entire area under water.

Photo courtesy the Northeast River Forecast Center

RIGHT: Extreme flooding in West Warwick, RI completely overwhelms a neighborhood.

Photo by Ellary Gamache

LEFT: An "angry ocean" in Rockport, Massachusetts during the March storm of 2010.

Photo by Katherine Davis

TOP, RIGHT: The Winooski River in Vermont runs over its banks and forces a road closure.
Photo courtesy Derek Maroot of Northeast Kingdom Weather

ABOVE, LEFT: Cars sitting in a flooded parking lot in Rhode Island. *Photo by Caitlin Mahoney*

ABOVE, RIGHT: Water takes over the streets during the March 2010 flooding. *Photo by Caitlin Mahoney*

Flooding from the March 2010 excessive rainfall. Ferry Park in Rocky Hill, CT., actually looks like it could use a ferry.

Photo by Dave Gilbert.

March 2010 Rhode Island eXtreme Flooding

Meteorologist Mark Searles, WJAR-TV, Providence, RI

In 16 years of forecasting New England weather, as well as nearly 40 years of living in the region, I have to say that the flood of March 2010 goes down as the single most incredible event I have witnessed. An amazing amount of rain (over sixteen inches) in one month, but what's more astounding is that almost ten inches of that fell in a little over a day & a half.

Now, just to set this up a bit, earlier in the month we had two other heavy rain events that caused local flooding problems. The ground was saturated from over seven inches of rain in two weeks' time so now there was simply nowhere for the water to go. Looking at the forecast guidance and seeing the potential of another six to ten inches of rain, I knew we were facing a potential disaster—but no one could possibly know how devastating the flooding would become.

One of the state's biggest watersheds, the Pawtuxet, had reached an historic crest earlier in the month of 14.98 feet. After receding below flood stage this same river would rise to an amazing 20.7-foot level after the rain ended on March 30th.

A feeling of utter helplessness came over Rhode Islanders as the rain continued to fall. Sights I never imagined flashed across our televisions sets: a large part of the state's main interstate route,I-95, shut down as water flooded both sides of the highway; one of the state's largest shopping malls completely flooded out; cars in the mall parking lot with water nearly up to their roofs! Water inside the mall flooding every single store; many would take months to re-open.

Unsanitary conditions abounded as many local sewer treatment plants were inundated, unable to keep up with the volume of water passing into the system as the river literally washed right through the treatment plants. You can imagine the volume of raw, untreated sewage rushing through area streets and homes!

The saddest stories were those told by lifelong residents of the state, those who never had flood waters in their homes in the decades they had lived there—but did now. A lifetime of memories washed away in an instant. The water would recede but the cleanup would be more than many could bear.

With their homes ruined, uninhabitable due to the presence of black mold, fecal coliform and mildew, some were forced to simply abandon, while others began the long, painstaking process of gutting and then rebuilding. A process which would take months if not longer.

Some called it a hundred year flood; others said it was more like a 500-year event. Many didn't care what it was called; they simply know it as "the flood." They say if it can happen once then it can certainly happen again!

The flood reminds me of how little data we actually have when it comes to weather history. We talk about "averages" and "normals"—information we have collected for about 100 years or so. Such a small sample, really, when you stop and think about it. What is really "normal" when it comes to our weather? As meteorologists it is our job to forecast the weather and sometimes we do so without giving much thought to the impact the day-to-day forecast might have on our community. The flood of March 2010 changed that somewhat, at least in the sense that it was a vivid reminder of how important weather is and the tremendous impact it has on our lives.

You can bet that in the years to come those of us who lived through the March 2010 flood will never forget what we saw, and how high the water rose. It's my hope that we use those memories productively and become better prepared. We can't stop the water from rising but perhaps we will remember how high it might get and take care to protect our valuables. I know I will always have an extra pump at the ready, just in case.

Just as the blizzard of '78 will live forever in many New Englanders' memory banks, so too will the flood of March 2010. We will never forget.

This poster is a part of a public information campaign to raise awareness of the dangers from flash floods.

Created by the NOAA

LEFT: A flooded street in Exeter, NH.
Photo courtesy Ed Bouras

BELOW: Route I-95 in Rhode Island had to be shut down when it flooded in March of 2010.
Photo by Catherine Tonsberg.

ABOVE: Water at the West Warwick Mall completely flooded the parking lot and made a shopping excursion impossible. *Photo courtesy the Northeast River Forecast Center*

BELOW: This Providence, RI motorist may have just flooded his engine.

On top of Mount Washington, you'd expect to have trouble walking into the wind. But when strong gusts happen elsewhere, it causes big problems. High winds can blow down trees, structures, and even fuel fires!

Photo courtesy the Mount Washington Observatory

CHAPTER 10: HIGH WINDS

Strong and dangerous winds are usually a symptom of a larger storm or weather system. As you're discovering, winds are part of many types of weather, and therefore are discussed in most chapters of this book. Downdrafts and microbursts come along with thunderstorms and hazardously strong gusts are a major force in tornadoes and hurricanes. Nor'easters quite often produce strong wind when they explode in power after reaching the Atlantic Ocean. Because of our proximity to the ocean, the northeast gets the "pleasure" of these winds quite often. This is one reason the tops of both Mount Washington in New Hampshire, and the Blue Hill Observatory in Massachusetts, see some of the windiest conditions in the US.

You be the Judge!	
QUESTION: Ancient Greeks used to think that wind was...	**QUESTION:** A "Zephyr" is...
A) The Earth breathing in and out.	A) A strong wind gust on Mars
B) The Gods getting angry.	B) A gentle breeze.
C) Because someone accidentally left a fan turned on.	C) A large blimp-like balloon.
ANSWER: A - They thought it was from planet Earth breathing in and out.	ANSWER: B - A gentle breeze between 3-7 miles per hour.

So, why does the wind scream so angrily around these storm systems? Well, the movement of air, which makes wind, is caused by air pressure differences. Low pressure sucks air into its center, it rises up into the atmosphere and exhausts out into the jet stream. When this happens, there is a continuous need for more and more air. The low pulls it in like a giant air vacuum cleaner, inhaling it from all around.

High pressure works almost the opposite way; it's almost like an atmospheric traffic jam in the jet stream. With too much air crammed in miles up in the sky, it sinks down to the ground and fans out all around. The more air that bunches up, the more air it must rid itself of.

As high pressure ejects all that extra air, low pressure is only too happy to inhale it. This air moving around from high to low pressure is what we call wind. The stronger the low or high pressure, the faster this process occurs, meaning the faster the wind speed.

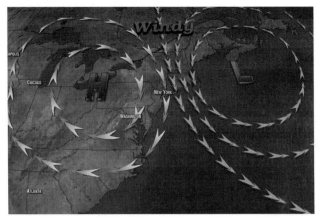

As the wind blows to and from high and how pressure, it circles around them because of the Earth's rotation (called "Coriolis Force"). Wind flows clockwise around areas of high pressure and counter-clockwise around low pressure.

Storms often undergo amazing transformations over the ocean to our east, becoming much mightier. Suddenly the low needs to bring in more air, and so the wind roars! Occasionally this happens as the storm is approaching, and much more often this happens as a storm is pulling away and gaining strength.

Fire Danger

When the wind is blowing, fire danger instantly goes up. If the weather has been dry, even for just a few days, the fire danger rises even higher. Think about it: what do you do when you're trying to get your fireplace going good?

You use a bellows and blow air at it, of course! When the wind blows on an outdoor fire, it acts as a giant bellows, and fans the flames. So while the wind doesn't always start the fire, it can help it quickly get out of control. There are times when the wind does start the fire, most often when it smashes combustible objects like fuel tanks.

It only takes a few rain-free days of nice weather for things to dry out enough to raise the fire danger. The ground doesn't need to be dry, just the leaves, sticks, and debris that are above the ground. When

Wind can quickly drive a fire out of control.

these dry out, fires become more likely. Add low humidity and the wind into the equation, and the fire risk goes up fast. Fire can be started by natural causes (like lightning), and by man. Either way, once it's started, the right weather conditions can cause it to grow out of control very fast.

The National Weather Service monitors these conditions closely and when the criteria are met, they issue fire weather watches and "Red Flag Warnings." Some of the important criteria they look for are:

- Air relative humidity levels below 30%

- Winds gusting to or above 25 miles per hour

- Rainfall amounts from the previous five days of under one quarter inch

Rating the Wind

Hundreds of years ago it was important for ships at sea to be able to classify what type of breeze was blowing, since they were powered by sails. The problem was, there was no standard wind scale that everyone used. One sailor might consider it to be windy, but another may think he was full of hot air and that it was just a little breezy. A scale needed to be developed so that everyone was "on the same page," so to speak. There were many variations created, but finally in the year 1805, Sir Francis Beaufort of England developed the version that became official. Since then, it has been adapted to keep it up to date, but is still called "The Beaufort Wind Scale" and is quite close to criteria used today by the National Weather Service. Originally created just for ships at sea, it has also been expanded for use on land as well.

Sir Francis Beaufort of England originated the "Beaufort Scale" in 1805.

Beaufort Wind Scale				
Force	Wind (mph)	WMO Classification	Appearance of Wind Effects	
			On the Water	On Land
0	Less than 1	Calm	Sea surface smooth and mirror-like	Calm; smoke rises vertically
1	1-3	Light Air	Scaly ripples, no foam crests	Smoke drift indicates wind direction; wind vanes still
2	4-7	Light Breeze	Small wavelets, crests glassy, no breaking	Wind felt on face, leaves rustle, vanes begin to move
3	8-12	Gentle Breeze	Large wavelets, crests begin to break, scattered whitecaps	Leaves and small twigs constantly moving, light flags extended
4	13-17	Moderate Breeze	Small waves, 1-4 ft, becoming longer, numerous whitecaps	Dust, leaves, and loose paper lifted, small tree branches move
5	18-24	Fresh Breeze	Moderate waves 4-8 ft taking longer form, many whitecaps, some spray	Small trees in leaf begin to sway
6	25-30	Strong Breeze	Larger waves 8-13 ft, whitecaps common, more spray	Larger tree branches moving, whistling in wires

			Beaufort Wind Scale (cont.)		
Force	Wind (mph)	WMO Classification	Appearance of Wind Effects		
			On the Water	On Land	
7	31-38	Near-Gale	Sea heaps up, waves 13-20 ft, white foam streaks off breakers	Whole trees moving, resistance felt walking against wind	
8	39-46	Gale	Moderately high (13-20 ft) waves of greater length, edges of crests begin to break into spindrift, foam blown in streaks	Whole trees in motion, resistance felt walking against wind	
9	47-54	Strong Gale	High waves (20 ft), sea begins to roll, dense streaks of foam, spray may reduce visibility	Slight structural damage occurs, slate blows off roofs	
10	55-63	Storm	Very high waves (20-30 ft) with overhanging crests, sea white with densely blown foam, heavy rolling, lowered visibility	Seldom experienced on land, trees broken or uprooted, considerable structural damage	
11	64-72	Violent Storm	Exceptionally high (30-45 ft) waves, foam patches cover sea, visibility more reduced		
12	73+	Hurricane	Air filled with foam, waves over 45 ft, sea completely white with driving spray, visibility greatly reduced		

Some of the strongest winds recorded in New England

- Mount Washington Observatory clocked wind at 231 mph on April 12, 1934, which remains the highest wind ever recorded in the northern and western Hemispheres
- Sustained five-minute wind of 121 mph with a gust to 186 mph during the Hurricane of 1938 at Blue Hill Observatory, Milton, MA.
- Wind gust of 135 mph in Hurricanes Carol (1954) and Donna (1960) on Block Island, RI.
- Sustained wind of 90 mph with a gust to 105 mph at Providence, RI in Hurricane Carol (1954)

Notable Windstorms and Stories

May 26, 1903 Windstorm Leads to Gigantic Lakeport, NH Fire: The weather had been very dry for much of May, and then came the wind storm. A fire, sparked by a boiler, broke out at H.H. Wood's mill, and quickly began to spread to other structures. Fire engineers telegraphed many surrounding towns for help as the fire grew quickly out of control. The flames were rapidly jumping building to building along Washington and Elm Streets as well as up Belvidere Hill. The fierce winds fanned the flames and allowed them to ignite every dry piece of tinder around.

Despite help arriving from neighboring Meredith and Tilton, as well as equipment arriving from Dover, Concord, and Franklin, the firefighters found that even their hoses were burnt!

The relentless winds even picked up lit fragments of burning buildings and blew them as much as four miles away, and then they lit other buildings on fire. What a mess, and firefighters were eventually forced to retreat.

By the end of the day there was little left but the charred remains of 108 houses, two mills, a lumber yard, several other businesses, and two churches. About 500 people were homeless and even farm animals were wandering around, aimlessly searching for the place they had called home.

A photo of the HH Wood Mill and Boulia-Gorrell Lumber Company buildings burning down during the Lakeport fire of 1903. At the right is the Bayside Mill.

Photo courtesy Laconia Historical and Museum Society, Inc., Laconia, NH

February 24-25th, 2010 Wind, Snow and Rain Storm: One of the things that stand out about this storm is that it brought quite a variety of weather types to the region. First, heavy snow covered portions of interior New England. One to two feet fell in western parts of Vermont, New Hampshire, and Massachusetts. Then the precipitation turned to rain, and a heavy rain it was, two to six inches worth with isolated higher amounts. As if New Englanders hadn't been through enough, next came the strong wind that night, for some the most powerful winds in many years. Highest gusts were felt in southern New Hampshire, southwestern Maine, and eastern Massachusetts. A buoy at the Isles of Shoals (just offshore from Portsmouth, NH) recorded a 91 mph wind gust, comparable to a strong category 1 hurricane. Damage in the hardest hit areas was widespread, and since the ground was soggy from the preceding precipitation, trees and other objects were toppled even more easily. In these hardest hit areas, over half a million people lost electricity for days, largely due to trees and poles being snapped. Roads were closed due to either flooding or downed trees, which made travel very frustrating.

The high winds fueled a fire that destroyed an entire block along Ocean Boulevard at Hampton Beach, NH including popular beach landmarks such as an arcade and restaurant.

Top Wind Gusts:

91 mph Isles of Shoals

78 mph Portland, ME

68 mph Portsmouth, NH

68 mph Concord, NH

67 mph Beverly, MA

63 mph Manchester, NH

63 mph Hudson, NH

61 mph Lawrence, MA

60 mph Boston, MA

52 mph Sanford, ME

50 mph Worcester, MA

A tree falls down in Manchester, New Hampshire, falling right onto the roof of this house. *Photo by Joseph Boell*

Winds over 60 mph toppled another tree, cutting into the roof of this house in Manchester, New Hampshire.

Photo by JC Haze

Strong winds fueled the flames of this fire, which completely destroyed this block of buildings on Hampton Beach. *Photos courtesy Ulocal.wmur.com*

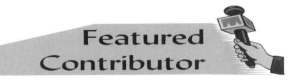

Featured Contributor

Hurricane Force Winds in Maine & NH

Meteorologist Tom Chisholm, WMTW-TV, Portland, ME

The vast and powerful ocean-born storm that battered New England from the 24th to 26th of February 2010 was the climactic event of an epoch winter. It was characterized by hurricane force winds, record-breaking rainfall, and astonishing snows that will live in family lore for years. Flooding was dreadful; a disaster to residents of Coastal and interior Maine and New Hampshire, home to my television audience. Locally, winds were astonishing, with winds gusting to 78 miles per hour in Portland, stronger than five notable hurricanes that affected the area. Nearby Cape Elizabeth was battered by a hurricane force wind of 94 miles per hour. Many homes were damaged or destroyed along coastal York County while scores of roads were washed out in central Cumberland County, where a narrow band of rainfall totaling over nine inches drenched the area.

The storm, one of four during the winter, evolved in an unusual manner. Ocean-born and to some extent deriving heat from the unusually warm waters of the north Atlantic, the powerful storm had a central pressure that rivals some tropical cyclones, with a central barometric pressure of about 966 millibars at its strongest (that's a very strong storm). It formed within the southern jet stream branch, the result of an El Niño event and was then blocked from an orderly advance to the North Atlantic by incredibly strong and blocking high pressure over Greenland. Astonishingly, as with the others that winter, the storm was forced to move from southeast to northwest carrying mild Atlantic air and amazing moisture far to the west and changed a heavy snowfall that began the storm to torrential rainfall in the mountains of northern New England. In the meantime, the geometry of the storm essentially inverted, bringing cold air to the southwest quadrant of the nor'easter and bringing crushing snowfalls to the Massachusetts Berkshires, where over two feet fell, and to about three feet in some New York City suburbs.

Ironically, to date Portland had only received six one hundredths of an inch of rain for the month. Yet the 5.75" of rain that fell on the 25th was the rainiest February day on record, going back to 1871.

ABOVE: Strong winds knock over large trees in Grand Island, Vermont. *Photo by Kay Trudell*

BELOW: Crews work to remove downed trees from strong winds in Vermont after the wind knocked them down in 2003.

Roof-less Radio!

By Heather Bishop

You would never think that a radio station on the fifth floor could get flooded during a wind storm, but it happened! It was the end of February 2010 and the wind and rains were blocking the signal for one of our stations, 96.5 The Mill. Our operations manager went into the building to see what was up and to get something on the air. While he was there he heard a horrible crash and then the fire alarms going off. Being a smart man, he ran! Soon the Manchester fire department was on the scene. As he and the fire fighters went up the stairs, water was pouring down the stairwell. He said it looked like a river running down from the fifth floor.

Come to find out, the front part of the building was an add-on. The two bathrooms on the Commercial Street side were added on later and had a different type of roof. The strong winds had ripped part of it off, and with it a sprinkler head burst open. Approximately 60,000 gallons of water poured out of that sprinkler and destroyed almost everything on our floor.

The devastation was massive. Almost every room had three or more inches of water in it, all except the main WZID studio. The building was uninhabitable; all but the on-air staff were moved to a temporary location in Merrimack where they stayed for months. Every wall had to be cut and air driers were brought in. The building temperature was up to 113° in an attempt to kill the mold spores. All of the floors were pulled up and taken down to the bare gypsum and in places you could see through to the fourth floor.

The ladies' room looks like it was hit by a tsunami. This is where most of the water entered, after the winds ripped off the roof.

Photo provided by WZID

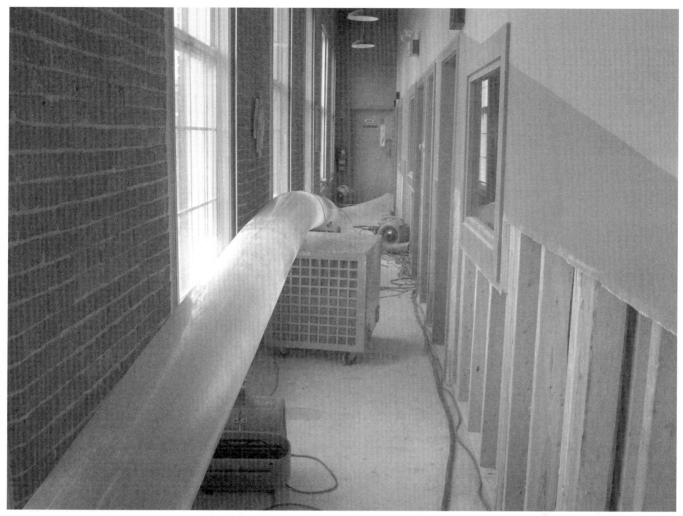

Blowers worked for months trying to dry out the air and tubes moved air around; walls and floors were stripped down to be replaced.

Photo provided by WZID

Definitely Dangerous Driving in the Wind Storm!

By Jean Fairbanks

I traveled from Walpole to Keene, NH, at midnight and was forced to get out of my 4-WD three times and remove small trees from Rte. 12A on the trek down. Then, going north just before 6 AM, I narrowly missed being hit by a huge tree that fell across and blocked Rte. 12 in Keene. Once in Walpole, I was detoured because of downed trees and power lines. I've driven in all kinds of weather, but the intensity of this particular storm made it perhaps one of my most dangerous trips, ever. Aside from having to get to work that night, being on the road at the height of the storm was just plain stupid.

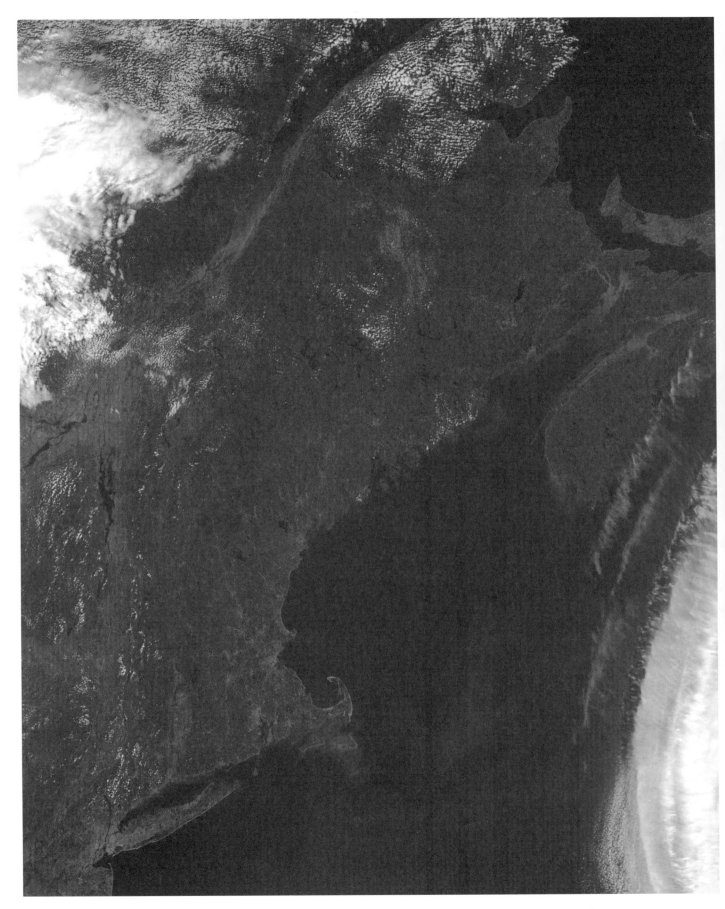

A satellite view shows clear skies over the northeastern United States. These pictures help government supercomputers produce the weather models that guide meteorologists.

CHAPTER 11: HOW DO METEOROLOGISTS PREDICT THE WEATHER?

Special thanks to John Kelley, Ph.D. Meteorologist, for writing this very interesting chapter of the book. Here is the "inside scoop" from the very people who make those "computer models" that you've always heard about, which help meteorologists forecast the weather.

Computer-Based Weather Forecast Models

By John G.W. Kelley, PhD. Meteorologist
NOAA/National Ocean Service/Coast Survey Development Lab/Marine Modeling and Analysis Programs

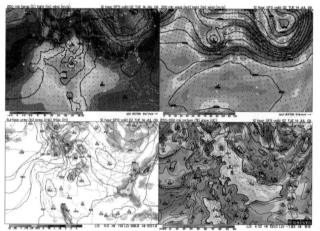

Did you ever wonder what TV weather forecasters mean when they say that our computer weather models are indicating a major nor'easter next week? What they are referring to are highly sophisticated numerical weather prediction models run on supercomputers at national weather forecast centers in the United States and around the world. Weather forecasts rely heavily on predictions from weather prediction models in creating their weather forecasts every day.

These weather forecast models consist of fundamental mathematical equations that govern the dynamics and thermodynamics of the Earth's atmosphere. The typical model represents the atmosphere as 30 to 40 layers extending from the surface into the middle stratosphere. The model equations are solved at specific locations on a computational grid or mesh covering a specific geographic area (e.g. United States) or the entire globe. The models include information about topography, land cover (e.g. forest, desert, lakes), and estimates of snow and ice cover. The model equations estimate future values of atmospheric variables such as air temperature, pressure, water vapor, wind speed and direction for several hours or many days in advance.

The model is started (or what meteorologists call "initialized") by assimilating observations of air temperature, dew point temperature, air pressure, wind direction and speed to describe the present three-dimensional structure of the atmosphere. These observations are obtained in near-real-time from weather stations, weather buoys, ships, weather satellites, weather radars, weather balloons, and commercial aircraft. Most models are run four times per day, initialized at 0000, 0600, 1200, and 1800 UTC or Greenwich Mean Time. These times were chosen since this is the time when there is the greatest number of observations available, especially above surface. In New England, these times correspond to 8 PM, 2 AM, 8 AM, and 2 PM EDT. The models do not start running right at these hours but wait for about one and half hours to receive and quality control observations from around the U.S., North America, and the world. Once the models start running it takes several hours for these model to finish even on the largest supercomputers in the world. Depending on the type, a model is run out to 18, 84, or 180 hours into the future, providing predictions every one or three hours to meteorologists. For example, a model covering North America called the North American Mesoscale (NAM) Model takes approximately one and a half hours to make forecasts out to 84 hours. Thus, a weather forecaster in New England will have to wait until about 1130 AM to see the predictions from the 1200 UTC model run.

Meteorologists in New England and in the rest of the U.S. rely on several weather models operated 24 x 7 by the U.S. government, the U.S. military, the national forecast centers of other counties, and private weather companies year-round. In the U.S., NOAA/National Weather Service (NWS) National Centers for Environmental Prediction (NCEP) (*http://www.ncep.noaa.gov*), located near Washington, DC, runs several forecast models including the NAM, the Global Forecast System, and the Rapid Update Cycle on a supercomputer. During the hurricane season, NCEP will also run two models, especially designed for forecasting individual tropical cyclones. These models utilize the latest observations from hurricane-hunter aircraft operated by the U.S. Air Force Reserves and NOAA. Given the importance of the predictions from these models to forecasters in the U.S. and around the world, NCEP operates a backup supercomputer in West Virginia in case the primary computer in metro DC fails, due to a power outage, for example.

The predictions from a weather models are commonly referred to as "forecast guidance" by meteorologists. The model predictions consist of numerical values of various atmospheric variables at each grid point on each model's layer, at hourly or 3-hour intervals. The output from the forecast models are disseminated to weather forecasters around the U.S and other countries as well. The numerical output from one model can take many gigabytes of storage. It would be impossible for a forecaster to examine the forecasts at each grid point and still make a forecast on time. Fortunately, computer graphical software converts these numerical values into colorful forecast maps of air temperature, wind speed and direction, dew point, at standard height or pressure levels (e.g. 500 millibars), as vertical soundings at selected locations, as vertical slices or cross sections, and even 3-D images. Weather forecasters carefully examine and compare the latest guidance from several forecast models and from previous model runs. On some days, the models agree well but sometimes there are major differences. Forecasters consider how well the various models have performed over the past several days, weeks, or even season to determine which model has the best track record and which ones have the worst. Forecasters also look for consistency in predictions from one model run to the next one. The more agreement between models as well as consistency between model runs, the greater confidence the forecaster has in using the guidance to form his or her forecast. In addition, some weather forecast models are run with slightly different initial conditions, a method called ensemble forecasting. This method provides the forecaster with an average or ensemble mean of the different model forecasts and probabilistic forecasts of future conditions.

To help the forecasters interpret the model forecasts in terms of surface weather (e.g. maximum and minimum temperatures) for a particular location, the NWS also provides predictions from a statistical method called Model Output Statistics. MOS relates observations of surface weather variables to model predictions as well as average climatic conditions and terrain and present conditions. Forecasters use the model guidance, MOS-based predictions, and their meteorological experience and knowledge of local effects to make their weather forecast.

Weather forecasters have relied on guidance from weather prediction models for over 50 years. The first operational numerical weather prediction in the U.S. began on July 1, 1954, by the Joint Numerical Weather Prediction Unit staffed by members of the U.S. Weather Bureau (the former name for the National Weather Service), the U.S. Air Force, and the U.S. Navy. Since then weather forecast models have improved considerably with advancements in computer technology, better understanding about weather systems from research, data from new observing systems and methods for assimilating these data, and the evolution of ensemble forecasting.

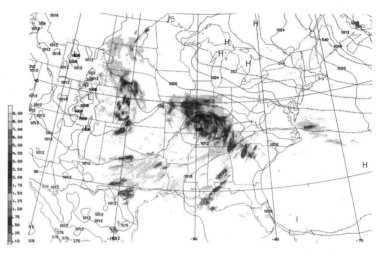

An actual map from a supercomputer model. As you can see, a storm is moving up through the Tennessee Valley, possibly headed for New England.

Image created by NCEP

The techniques of numerical prediction have been extended to forecasting ocean waves, currents, water temperature, water levels and salinity and also air quality. NOAA's Ocean Service now operates numerical ocean forecast models for predicting water levels, currents, water temperature, and salinity in seaports, estuaries, and the Great Lakes. Some weather forecast models designed for tropical cyclones are now coupled with ocean forecast models to take into account the impact of ocean water temperature and wave heights on intensification and movement of tropical storms.

NCEP's weather forecast models are continually being improved by research meteorologists located at NCEP's Environmental Modeling Center, other parts of NOAA, and at universities. Weather forecasters can expect significant improvements in NOAA's forecast models in the coming years, which should lead to better model guidance to help make their forecast for today or next week.

NCEP supercomputers do what no team of humans could possibly do.
Photo courtesy NCEP

ABOVE: The super computers of NCEP are so big, they take up an entire room.

Photo courtesy NCEP

LEFT: A typical scene at most any National Weather Service office, this one in Gray, Maine. The NWS analyzes all the data from the supercomputer models and develops their forecast.

Photo by John Jensenius

A weather balloon being released in Gray, Maine. It travels miles up into the sky and relays hundreds of readings back, providing information for the weather computer models. Hundreds of other balloons are simultaneously released all over the continent.

Photos by John Jensenius

The Blue Hill Observatory in Milton, Massachusetts during the early winter

CHAPTER 12: HOW WEATHER OBSERVATIONS SERVE YOU

The Blue Hill Observatory

The Blue Hill Observatory in Milton, Massachusetts is the oldest continuously operating weather observatory in the United States. The first observations were taken on February 1, 1885. Since that date, observers have been using the same methods, following the same protocols, and using the same types of instruments (in some cases, they still use the original instruments) to record every aspect of the weather on top of Great Blue Hill. Because they have not made any significant changes in how they record the weather, the Observatory is the home of the oldest  homogeneous weather and climate record in the nation. On February 1, 2010 the Observatory celebrated 125 years of continuous weather observations.

The Observatory is now operated by the Blue Hill Observatory Science Center, a nonprofit organization whose mission is to maintain the weather observation program as well as to offer unique educational programs to thousands of guests every year. Their continued operation is made possible by generous donations from members, friends, corporations, and foundations. For more information about the Blue Hill Observatory, or to learn how you can contribute or schedule a visit, please visit their website: *http://www.bluehill.org.*

Here are a few significant events in the Observatory's history:

- February 1, 1885: First observations made by Willard P. Gerrish and Abbott Lawrence Rotch.

- September 21, 1938: The highest recorded wind gust during a hurricane was measured (calculated gust 186 MPH). Sustained winds of 121 MPH for 5 minutes were also observed during the 1938 hurricane.

- June 9, 1953: Shingles, letters, and other assorted debris fell down on Blue Hill from the Worcester Tornado. Observer John Conover talked with Ken McCasland, who was at Woods Hole, and noted the tops of the clouds from that powerful storm were visible from Cape Cod.

- October 1960: Chief Observer Robert Skilling started work at Blue Hill Observatory. Bob is still observing in the 21st century, and celebrated 50 years at the Observatory in October 2010.

- February 1, 2010: Blue Hill Observatory celebrates 125 years of continuous weather observations. Chief Observer Robert Skilling performs observer's duties for the day.

125-Year climatological data & records from The Blue Hill Meteorological Observatory		
Milton, MA - Elevation 635 ft.		
EVENT	RECORD	DATE
Average Annual Temperature:	47.5 deg F	
Average Annual Precipitation:	48.58 inches	
Precipitation Annual Maximum:	71.00 inches	1998
Average Seasonal Snowfall:	60.7 inches	
Snowfall 24-hour Maximum:	29.0 inches	3/31– 4/1/1997
Snowfall Seasonal Maximum:	144.4 inches	1995-1996
Greatest 24-hour Rainfall:	9.93 inches – Hurricane Diane	1955
Greatest Monthly Rainfall:	18.81 inches	March 2010
Average Wind Speed and Direction:	14.9 mph, W	
Highest Temperature:	101 deg F	8/2/1975
Lowest Temperature:	-21 deg F	2/9/1934
Highest Wind:	186 mph	9/21/1938
Highest Barometer:	31.08 inches Hg	
Lowest Barometer:	28.42 inches Hg	

How you can Become a Weather Spotter

So, have you always wondered how you could become an "official" weather spotter? Or perhaps this book has inspired you. There are two ways you can relay your information to meteorologists, which can put your city or town, literally, on the map!

First off, you can contact your local TV meteorologist (many of them have contributed stories to this book). Most television weather departments welcome your snow and rainfall amounts, wind measurements, high/low temperatures, storm damage, and more. Visit the website for your favorite local TV station and you'll most likely find a link to where you can e-mail your reports and perhaps get them on TV.

Secondly, check out organizations like the Community Collaborative Rain, Hail & Snow Network. These organizations collect data and distribute it on the web. You can find out more and also view their data at: *www.cocorahs.org*

Finally, the National Weather Service's SKYWARN program trains volunteers to become official spotters. The reports you make to the NWS help them decide where to issue warnings, and also go into the official weather records. TV weathercasters frequently use this information, along with other public and government agencies. If you'd like to be trained to become a SKYWARN spotter, visit your local NWS webpage for details.

- NWS Boston (Massachusetts, Rhode Island, Connecticut, southwest New Hampshire): *www.erh.noaa.gov/box*

- NWS Gray, ME (The southern half of Maine, and most of New Hampshire, except Hillsborough and Cheshire Counties): *www.erh.noaa.gov/gyx*

- NWS Caribou (Northern half of Maine): *www.erh.noaa.gov/car*

- NWS Vermont (all of Vermont): *www.erh.noaa.gov/btv*

Watches, Warnings and Advisories

When extreme and/or dangerous weather is observed, predicted or imminent, the National Weather Service, Storm Prediction Center, and National Hurricane Center, issue various types of statements to warn the public. They are passed along by TV meteorologists and others because of their extreme importance. The criteria differ depending on where you live. Areas that are used to seeing more of one type of weather have higher thresholds before these warnings are issued. For example, down in southern parts of the United States, the mere possibility of an inch of snow causes warnings and advisories to be declared. Meanwhile, it takes snow predictions of at least six inches before similar warnings are issued in New England. What follows are the different types, as well as what they mean, and when they are issued.

Weather can be very dangerous, like this road. So always listen when there is a weather advisory!

Photo by Terri Trier

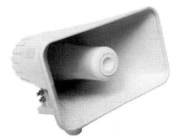

Type of Issuance

Winter Weather Advisory: When any of the following is expected within the next 12 to 24 hours:

- A winter weather event that meets or exceeds advisory criteria, but which remains below warning criteria.

- Snow, Ocean Effect Snow, and/or Sleet

    - 3 inches averaged over a CT, MA, RI forecast zone in 12 hours

    - 4 inches averaged over a NH, VT, ME forecast zone in 12 hours

Snow and Blowing Snow: Sustained or frequent gusts of 25 to 34 mph accompanied by falling and blowing snow occasionally reducing visibility to $\leq$ ¼ mi for $\geq$ 3 hours.

Blowing Snow: Widespread or localized blowing snow reducing visibility to $\leq$ ¼ mi with winds < 35 mph.

Black Ice: A Special Weather Statement will usually be issued when sufficient moisture is expected to cause a thin layer of ice on road surfaces, typically on cloudless nights ("black ice"). At forecaster discretion, a formal Winter Weather Advisory may be issued instead.

Winter Storm Warning: When any of the following is expected within the next 12 to 36 hours:

- Winter weather event meeting or exceeding warning criteria for at least one of the precipitation elements:

- Snow, Ocean Effect Snow, or Sleet

    - 6 inches averaged over a forecast zone in a 12 hour period *-or-*

    - 8 inches averaged over a CT, MA, RI forecast zone in a 24 hour period

    - 9 inches averaged over a NH, VT, ME forecast zone in a 24 hour period

Blizzard Warning: Sustained winds or frequent gusts > 35 mph and considerable falling and/or blowing snow frequently reducing visibility less than ¼ mile for at least 3 hours Blizzard conditions need to be the *predominant condition over a 3 hour period.*

Freezing Rain Advisory: Any accretion of freezing rain or freezing drizzle on road surfaces.

Ice Storm Warning: One-half inch or greater accretion of freezing rain expected.

Wind Chill Advisory: Wind chill index between -15°F and -24°F (For MA, CT, and RI) and -20°F and -29°F (For NH, VT, and ME) for at least 3 hours *using only the sustained wind.*

Wind Chill Warning: Wind chill index of at least -25°F (for MA, CT, and RI) and -30°F (NH, VT, and ME) for at least 3 hours using only sustained wind.

Wind Advisory: Sustained winds 31-39 mph for at least 1 hour; OR any gusts to 46-57 mph.

High Wind Warning: Sustained winds 40-73 mph for at least 1 hour; OR any gusts ≥ 58 mph.

Hurricane Force Wind Warning: Sustained winds or frequent gusts ≥ 73 mph for > 2 hrs within 24 hours *from a non-tropical system.*

Tropical Storm Warning: Sustained winds 39-73 mph (no gust criteria) *associated with a tropical storm* expected to affect a specified coastal zone within 24 hours.

Tropical Storm Wind Warning (Inland): Sustained winds 39-73 mph (no gust criteria) *associated with a tropical storm* affecting areas beyond coastal zone (inland) within 24 hours.

Hurricane Watch: An announcement that hurricane force winds are *possible* within the specified coastal area. Because hurricane preparedness activities become difficult once winds reach tropical storm force, the hurricane watch is issued 48 hours in advance of the anticipated onset of tropical-storm-force winds.

Hurricane Warning: Sustained winds ≥ 74 mph (no gust criteria) *associated with a hurricane* expected to affect a specified coastal area within 24 hours.

Hurricane Wind Warning (Inland): Sustained winds ≥ 74 mph (no gust criteria) *associated with a hurricane* affecting areas beyond coastal zone (inland) within 24 hours

Severe Thunderstorm Watch: Outlines an area where an organized episode of hail one inch diameter or larger and/or damaging thunderstorm winds are expected or possible during a three to eight hour period.

Severe Thunderstorm Warning: Thunderstorms with wind gusts ≥ 58 mph and/or hail ≥ 1" in diameter.

Tornado Watch: These are issued when weather conditions are favorable for the development of tornadoes in and close to the watch area. Tornado watches also include the chance of organized large hail and damaging wind threats. Typical watches cover large areas, often half the size of a state.

Tornado Warning: Likelihood of a tornado within the given area based on radar or actual sighting; usually accompanied by conditions indicated above for "Severe Thunderstorm Warning."

Flood Advisory: Expected inundation of some low lying and poor drainage areas, resulting in a nuisance to the public but not a threat to life and property.

Flash Flood Warning: Rapid and extreme flow of high water into a normally dry area, or a rapid water level rise in a stream or creek above a predetermined flood level, beginning within a short timeframe from the onset of heavy rain. A dam or levee failure, or water released from an ice jam is also considered.

Flood Warning: Expected overflow or inundation by water which causes or will cause damage and/or a threat to life.

River Flood Warning: Water level at a River Forecast point along a main stem river is expected to reach or exceed flood stage.

Coastal Flood Advisory: Minor coastal flooding expected within 12 hours. Examples include: splash over, causing a few roads to be briefly impassable, standing water in parking lots, etc.

Coastal Flood Warning: Coastal flooding expected within 12 hours; widespread serious coastal flooding which damages property and/or is a threat to life.

Heat Advisory: Daytime heat indices of 100°F-104°F for two or more hours.

Heat Wave: Issued for non-criteria warning/advisory heat. A heat wave is defined as three or more days of $\geq$ 90°F temperatures.

Excessive Heat Warning: Daytime heat indices of $\geq$ 105°F for two or more hours.

Dense Fog Advisory: Widespread visibility $\leq$ ¼ mile for at least three hours.

Freezing Fog Advisory: Very light ice accumulation from predominantly freezing fog.

Frost Advisory: Issued under clear, light wind conditions with forecast minimum shelter temperature 33-36°F during growing season.

Freeze Warning: When minimum shelter temperature drops to < 32°F during growing season.

High Surf Advisory: When high surf poses a danger to life in the form rip currents or breaking seas.

Fire Weather Watch: This means that critical fire weather conditions are forecast to occur. Listen for later forecasts and possible red flag warnings.

Red Flag Warning: High degree of confidence that dry fuels and weather conditions support extreme fire danger within 24 hours using the following criteria as a guide:

- Winds sustained or with frequent gusts $\geq$ 25 mph

- Relative Humidity at or below 30% anytime during the day

- Rainfall amounts for the previous 5 days less than 0.25 inches (except 3 days in pre-greenup)

- Lightning after an extended dry period

- Significant dry frontal passage

- Dry thunderstorms

New England Weather Extremes State Records			
Source: Northeast National Climatic Data Center			
Connecticut			
24-hour precipitation:	Burlington	12.77"	August 19, 1955
24-hour snowfall:	Falls Village	30"	February 10, 1969
Snow Depth:	Norfolk	55"	February 5, 1961
Maximum Temperature:	Torrington	106°	August 23, 1916
	Danbury	106°	July 15, 1995
Minimum Temperature:	Falls Village	-32 °	January 5, 1904
	Coventry	-32 °	February 15, 1943
Maine			
24-hour precipitation:	Portland	13.32"	October 20-21, 1996
24-hour snowfall:	Orono	40"	December 30, 1962
Snow Depth	Farmington	84"	February 28, 1969
Maximum Temperature:	North Bridgton	105°	July 4 & 10, 1911
Minimum Temperature:	Big Black River	-50°	January 16, 2009
Massachusetts			
24-hour precipitation:	Westfield	18.15"	August 18-19, 1955
24-hour snowfall:	Natick	29"	April 1, 1997
Snow Depth:	Great Barrington	62"	January 13, 1996
Maximum Temperature:	New Bedford	107°	August 2, 1975
	Chester	107°	August 2, 1975
Minimum Temperature:	Taunton	-35 °	January 5, 1904
	Coldbrook	-35 °	February 15, 1943
	Chester	-35 °	January 12, 1981

New England Weather Extremes State Records *(cont.)*

Source: Northeast National Climatic Data Center

New Hampshire

24-hour precipitation:	Mt. Washington	11.07"	October 20-21, 1996
24-hour snowfall:	Mt. Washington	49.3"	February 25, 1969
Snow Depth:	Pinkham Notch	164"	February 27, 1969
Maximum Temperature:	Nashua	106°	July 4, 1911
Minimum Temperature:	Mt. Washington	-46.5°	January 8, 1968

Rhode Island

24-hour precipitation:	Westerly	12.13"	September 16-17, 1932
24-hour snowfall:	Woonsocket	30"	February 7, 1978
Snow Depth:	North Foster	42"	February 7, 1978
Maximum Temperature:	Providence	104°	August 2, 1975
Minimum Temperature:	Wood River Junction	-28 °	January 11, 1942

Vermont

24-hour precipitation:	Mt. Mansfield	9.92"	September 17, 1999
24-hour snowfall:	Jay Peak	42"	February 5, 1995
Snow Depth	Mt. Mansfield	149"	April 2, 1969
Maximum Temperature:	Vernon	107°	July 7, 1912
Minimum Temperature:	Bloomfield	-50°	December 30, 1933

Josh's Top Ten Weather Myths

#10: A "100-year flood" only happens once every one hundred years

#9: A nor'easter is a storm that comes from the northeast.

#8: The bigger the hurricane, the stronger it is.

#7: Your vehicle is the safest place to be during a thunderstorm because of the rubber tires.

#6: Tornadoes cause more deaths than any other type of weather.

#5: It has never snowed in New England after June 1st.

#4: Lightning comes from the clouds down to the ground.

#3: Sleet and hail are basically the same thing

#2: Tornadoes almost never strike New England.

#1: A person struck by lightning is "electrically charged" and should not be touched.

Conclusion

I sincerely hope you've enjoyed reading about extreme weather in New England and how it occurs. These storms are very complicated, but perhaps you now have a little more insight into their makeup.

The weather keeps on happening, so there will be plenty more storms where these came from. My hope is that whenever you are affected (or about to be affected) by any type of extreme weather, perhaps you'll think to pull out this book and re-read that chapter to refresh your mind. Not only will you be more informed, but you may even be reminded of an important safety tip or two.

You also now have a handy reference to some of the biggest storms in the last 100 or so years here in New England. As mentioned earlier, it's impossible to mention them all, but it was very enjoyable to compile as many of them as I could into one place. The stunning pictures of past storms are a strong reminder of the power of the weather. The storm re-caps also make for great discussion starters with practically anyone.

Thanks for reading, and feel free to drop me a line with any comments or questions at: joshjudgeweather@gmail.com

Josh Judge

Websites Mentioned in the Book

Winter Weather Awareness

www.nws.noaa.gov/om/winter/index.shtml

Doppler Radar

www.radar.weather.gov

Lightning Safety

www.lightningsafety.noaa.gov

Lightning Strike & Electric Shock Survivors International, Inc

www.lightning-strike.org

Real Time River Flood Gauges

www.weather.gov/ahps

Storm Prediction Center

www.spc.noaa.gov

Air Quality

www.airnow.gov

National Hurricane Center

www.nhc.noaa.gov

Upcoming Hurricane Names

http://www.aoml.noaa.gov/hrd/tcfaq/B2.html

Retired Hurricane Storm Names

www.nhc.noaa.gov/retirednames.shtml

National Centers for Environmental Prediction

www.ncep.noaa.gov